ASSASSIN HUNTER

by

August Palumbo

ASSASSIN HUNTER

Copyright © 2012
by
August Palumbo

Published by

Southern Oaks Publishing
SouthernOaksPublishing@hotmail.com

ISBN-13: 9781470178741
ISBN-10: 1470178745

This material is copyrighted. No part of this book may be copied in any manner, electronically or otherwise, without the expressed permission of the author.

This story is based on a recount of real events. Some of the names have been changed to protect the living.

Assassin Hunter

Certainly there is no hunting like the hunting of man, and those who have hunted armed men long enough and liked it, never care for anything else thereafter.
- Ernest Hemingway

Assassin Hunter

Dedication

To my family, who endured the stress and pain of my undercover life.

Preface

ATF public relations personnel often stand alongside United States Attorneys and defer press releases to them. The sweeping jurisdiction of the agency and enforcement of unpopular laws has until recently kept ATF low profile in its perception, despite the hard-hitting and vital nature of its work. This policy has fostered the question, "Who are these guys?" as the jumpsuits emblazoned with ATF swarm over bomb scenes and storm buildings with search warrants.

Special Agents of the United States Justice Department's Bureau of Alcohol, Tobacco, Firearms and Explosives evolved from the first Treasury Agents appointed in 1789, and coalesced into one of the most eclectic, preeminent, and least-understood arms of federal law enforcement. They have been handed down the tradition of the first agents who battled pirates and smugglers with sabers and protected gold shipments. These agents were around more than one hundred and forty years before the creation of the Federal Bureau of Investigation. For a hundred years after the Civil War, scores of agents were killed and wounded as they fought bootleggers and moonshiners in the South in the bloodiest resistance to federal law enforcement in our history. Today's agents are also the successors of the Bureau of Prohibition agents, whose mission was to destroy violent criminal empires, and today they carry on the crime-busting duties of those "Untouchables." The agency was transferred from Treasury to the Justice Department amid the reorganization of federal law enforcement agencies in the wake of the 9/11 terrorist attacks.

ATF agents received accolades for their investigative work in the 1995 bombing of the Murrah federal building in Oklahoma City, as well as the 1993 bombing and 2001 attacks on the World Trade Center in New York. The ATF investigation of the 1996 Atlanta Olympics bombing and the 1998 abortion clinic bombing which took the life of a Birmingham police officer led to the indictment of Eric Robert Rudolph, who remained a federal fugitive for five years. They also received criticism from congressional committees and the press for their raid on David Koresh and his Branch Davidian compound in Waco, Texas in 1994. Four ATF agents were killed in the gun battle that followed their execution of a federal search warrant at that compound. Equal criticism fell on the agency for its part in the attempt to arrest Randy Weaver in Ruby Ridge, Idaho in 1992, which ultimately resulted in the deaths of Weaver's wife and son. The most recent criticism centers upon the bureau's 2011 gunrunning probe known as Operation Fast and Furious, in which ATF allowed firearms dealers to sell weapons to drug cartels through straw purchases. This allegedly resulted in the murder of U.S. Border Patrol agent Brian Terry by means of an illegally purchased AK-47. The family of the fallen officer has filed a $25 million wrongful death lawsuit against ATF. One senior congressman has publicly referred to ATF agents as "jack-booted thugs." Moreover, ATF is under constant scrutiny by gun advocates who believe the Bureau's regulation and enforcement of firearm laws abridges the Second Amendment right to bear arms.

Against this drumbeat of adversity, ATF agents have always been in the trenches of the war against crime, and they live daily with violence of every degree. Their mission to uncover illegal explosives has also catapulted them to the front lines against terrorism. The most intrepid and resourceful agents work undercover, known unofficially within the agency as *assassin hunters*. The laws they enforce address the most devious, violent, and menacing of criminals, and by their nature are often transgressed by organized groups and conspirators. This is underscored by the fact that the average federal prison term for criminals arrested and prosecuted by ATF nearly doubles the prison term for those brought to justice by the FBI.[1]

Historically, armed radical groups of the Left and the Right have been targets of ATF investigations, including the Black Panthers and the Ku Klux Klan. Organizations with sinister names such as The Order, Covenant of the Sword, Born to Kill, and Hell's Angels have been infiltrated by ATF undercover agents. Terrorists, mafia families, drug cartels, self-proclaimed militia units, motorcycle and street gangs, as well as the most dangerous individual and career criminals, have all felt the sting of ATF clandestine operations.

This book is based on a true personal account of one of those operations.

---

[1] TRAC, Syracuse University, 1999

Assassin Hunter

Prologue

Thirty-one year old patrolman Bobby Cazale' stood with his squad and stared intently at the unfamiliar light show set against the black sky. He wore the dark blue uniform well on his lean six-foot frame. When his fellow officers had exhausted their speculation on the source of the light, he said in a teasing but prophetic voice, "Maybe the end is near."

Twelve hours later he would be dead in a muzzle flash of flesh, bone and blood.

The detachment of police officers broke roll call and slowly flooded the shadowy parking lot of the New Orleans Police Department Seventh Precinct. The cool night air seemed to energize the group after they'd sat through the monotonous nightly meeting where they received their patrol assignments and listened to the desk sergeant drone through the previous day's crimes. They ambled toward the squad cars handed off from the previous watch, and loaded tools of the trade – shotguns, flashlights, briefcases

- into the vehicles that would be their homes and offices for the next eight hours. The routine was interrupted when several of them noticed a strange, reddish-orange glow in the distance. The light pulsated erratically with long, bright orange flashes, followed by staccato bursts of red tinged in low shades of blue.

The officers paused to look at the unexplained electrified sky painting. Their nickel-plated badges, nameplates, and weapons glinted in beat with the throbbing light. A few suggested that the light issued from a crew of arc welders working the night shift on the deck of a large Navy ship under construction at the Avondale Shipyard. One sergeant, an older veteran of the precinct, conjectured that the light emanated from one of the perpetual gas afterburners at the oil refineries located on the west bank of the Mississippi River. A young rookie quipped that the light might be a UFO.

That night Cazale' finished the uneventful tour of duty on the graveyard shift and hurried home. He had just enough time to see his twin daughters off to school and maybe catch a catnap before heading to his moonlighting job at the Commerce Bank and Trust Company of Louisiana. His wife had already left for work as a department store clerk, so he ushered the children to the corner and waited with them for the school bus. With no time for a nap he shaved and threw on a clean, starched, light blue uniform shirt ironed with military creases. He gulped a cup of coffee while reading the morning newspaper headlines, then headed to the bank which used off-duty police officers for security. He needed the extra income and had used his five years police experience to land the second job.

The stately old bank's two-story high ceiling and granite floors allowed for echoes in the lobby, which made most of the customers whisper as if in a church. Several tall Roman columns that supported the high ceiling were dispersed throughout the large room. Skylights blended with great fluorescent fixtures to throw an eerie, subdued light throughout the bank. A row of tellers stood behind a long marble counter with brass bars positioned between them and the customers in line, who held soft conversations with them as they conducted business. Marble trimmed the islands where people filled out deposit and transaction slips. An occasional clip-clop of high heels rose above the general murmurs. The building seemed to engulf and overwhelm anyone entering for the first time, and the combination of marble and acoustics gave it the ambience of a mausoleum.

The bank had been open a half-hour when Bobby Cazale' circulated among the bank officers and employees working the desks on the far side of the lobby. Behind the floor desks was a massive stainless steel vault containing safe deposit boxes and the bank's cash reserves and securities.

He had opened the bank most mornings for the past year and was familiar with the routine and all the employees. He chatted briefly with several workers, and had his back turned to the front entrance when two men quick-stepped through the large revolving brass doors. Their faces were grotesque and disfigured from stockings that were pulled down over their heads, and they brandished large caliber handguns.

The first through the door had a muscular build emphasized by tight-fitting blue jeans and a black t-shirt that fit snugly around his chest and arms. His partner was somewhat taller and dressed the same way, except that he wore cowboy boots that shuffled along the granite floor. As if drawn by a magnet, the first man moved toward Cazale' with a blue steel .9mm automatic pistol raised high in his right hand. The cowboy boots made their way to the teller line. A petite young loan officer, smartly dressed and wearing several rings on her fingers, was seated at a desk facing the entrance. Her body jumped as she looked up to see the gunman raise the automatic. She pointed the ringed fingers and called out to Cazale'. The officer instinctively unholstered his .357 magnum caliber service weapon, and with his gun drawn, turned to face the man. Cazale' got off three shots in a bizarre firefight. One bullet lodged in the robber's left side. A simultaneous fusillade of rounds came from the .9mm, one of which struck Cazale' in his forehead above the left eye. Blood and tissue splattered onto the desk and wall behind him as his body thrust back, and what was left of his head landed on the hard floor with a thud. Blood immediately drained from his wound and formed a large crimson pool under his head and upper body. His eyes were dilated and fixed open in a macabre stare. The cavernous lobby reverberated from the deafening and frightening noise made by the hail of gunfire.

The killer then moved with military precision toward the doors of the vault. He grabbed a bespectacled junior vice-president who was crouched behind a desk holding a canvas bank bag that contained bonds and negotiable securities. He stuck the automatic into the banker's neck and wrenched the bag from his hands, then ran to the teller cages where his partner had forced the employees to lie on the floor. The team emptied the cages and hurriedly shoved the cash into another canvas bag, then ran out of the lobby through the heavy brass revolving doors with a force that spun them around rapidly. The killer clutched his side and dripped a trail of blood from the wound inflicted by the fallen officer. The only sounds in the bank were the echoed cries and whimpers of the customers and bank employees who lay on the floor, though their ears still rang from the report of the loud gunshots. The entire incident had lasted only a couple of minutes.

Days later...

A vintage, dark blue Thunderbird with dark tinted glass rumbled up the incline of the emergency ramp at Our Lady of the Lake Hospital. A young attendant stepped on the rubber mat that opened the automatic glass doors. Dressed in a starched white uniform and white buck shoes, he selected one of the wheelchairs lined up on the ramp near the door. He wheeled the chair in the direction of the car, whose engine was still running. The orderly reached from behind the chair to open the passenger door and assist whoever was there for medical attention. With his fingers only inches from the handle, the door blasted open on its own, and a crumpled, bloody body tumbled out onto the driveway. Before the orderly could react, the T-bird's engine roared and the car raced down the ramp and out of sight.

"Stat!" he yelled to anyone in earshot. The night triage nurse, a fair-skinned blonde with pinned-up hair, scurried outside to assist. She knelt over the injured man, who lay on his side in the fetal position. Blood oozed through his fingers pressed against his left side, and his breathing was labored. He moaned in pain, and drifted in and out of consciousness as the nurse pried his hand away. She tore open his blood-drenched shirt, which exposed a makeshift bandage of drugstore-grade gauze and tape. The man was feverish with sweat beads formed on his forehead.

"Can you hear me?" she shouted.

The man responded, and he turned his head toward her. His dark eyes were half-dilated, and he had several days of beard growth on his face. "Yeah," he grunted.

"What's wrong? What kind of injury do you have?"

His eyes were now more attentive and fixed on her, but he gave no response.

"Answer me!" she demanded.

He remained silent, except for a few moans. More emergency room personnel arrived, including a thirty-one year old trauma resident. He conferred with the nurse, and satisfied that there were no other wounds or injuries, flipped the man on his back. The nurse and an orderly placed him onto a gurney that sprung up waist high, and rolled him into the green-tiled emergency room where an ER team took over from the triage nurse. They checked his vital signs and started an I.V. while the doctor slowly peeled the crude bandage from the patient's side, revealing a one-inch hole between the bottom ribs. From the dozens he had previously treated, he recognized it as a gunshot wound. "Bag this," he said, handing the bandage to a nurse, "it may be evidence."

Doctor Rudy Martinez, the senior trauma resident in the ER, spoke with a slight hint of Hispanic accent. His soft brown eyes blended with his dark, curly, close-cropped hair and there was a slight cleft in his chin. "Who shot you?" he directed at his patient. The man on the gurney gave the doctor a hard look. No answer. "Look, we're stabilizing you. We'll x-ray the area to be sure, but I don't think the bullet destroyed any vital organs. There's no exit wound, and you've got infection causing high fever. That means you're still carrying a bullet. If you don't talk to me, I can't help you. At least tell me when this happened."

"Three, maybe four days ago," a strained voice answered, "I passed out a few times so I'm not sure."

"What kind of gun was it?"

"You'll have to find out for yourself, Doc. That's all I'm telling you. Now gimme something for the pain."

Martinez was a veteran of the ER, no stranger to the carnage inflicted by man's inhumanity to man. He knew from the patient's demeanor and from the nature of the wound that he was more than a victim. Without waiting for the x-ray confirmation of a gunshot wound, he instructed the ER clerk to notify the Baton Rouge Police Department. The patient stabilized from the infusion of antibiotics, and from the procedures to ease breathing and stop the bleeding. Now hooked up to a respirator, monitors, and the I.V. that pumped painkillers, the patient went into a deep sleep.

Doctor Martinez sat in a small swivel chair and slapped the x-rays onto a light board. He guided a mug of strong black coffee to his lips, and wondered if by some remote chance the beans were harvested from his family's coffee plantation in his native Guatemala. He had studied medicine at NYU and interned at Roosevelt Hospital in New York, hoping for a residency at the famed Ochsner Clinic in New Orleans. His father had been a friend of the clinic's founder, who was also an activist for human rights in Central and South America. Misspent opportunities and a less than brilliant performance in medical school precluded any hope of residency at Ochsner, but he landed closeby at the well-respected Our Lady of the Lake. He enjoyed the subtropical climate of south Louisiana that was similar to his homeland. He also enjoyed working in the ER, the very same where U.S. Senator Huey Long was rushed from the state capitol for treatment in 1935, in a futile attempt to save his life after being shot by an assassin. Martinez had just been offered a permanent staff position at OLL and would probably accept the job.

He turned his attention back to the dark, opaque images illuminated in front of him. A medium caliber bullet, completely intact except for a small floating fragment near its nose, was lodged against the inside of the fourth rib. Unless the bullet moved, it was no immediate danger, except for infection. He was interrupted by a student nurse carrying a patient chart. "Excuse me, doctor, but we have a problem," she squeaked.

"What is it?"

"The patient in ER3, gunshot wound. He won't give us his name. What should I put on the chart and on his wristband?"

"John Doe," he answered. "Have the police arrived?"

"Yes, there's two uniformed officers with him."

Martinez finished his coffee and stepped to ER3, ignoring a page from the hospital intercom. Two uniformed cops, a man-woman team, stood on either side of the patient's gurney. "Did he give you any information?" he asked.

The male officer, apparent senior of the team answered, "No, sir. He won't talk to us. We can't do much here except guard him. I've notified the dick's office, they're sending someone over."

Martinez continued with other duties. He finished the last suture on the freckled forehead of a three-year-old girl who had rolled out of bed and struck her head on a night table. He softly hummed a Latino lullaby to calm her during the procedure. The student nurse interrupted once more. "Doctor, Sergeant Morrell is here to see you."

"Show him to my quarters, will you please?"

Detective Sergeant Frank Morrell waited in the small, Spartan room that Martinez used to steal naps in the middle of mayhem during his long shifts. He thumbed through some recent photos scattered on a small desk. They showed laborers picking coffee beans under a hot sun. One of them was of Rudy Martinez smiling while he gripped a thatched basket under his arms. Morrell paced slowly in the cluttered room. He was only months away from ending a thirty-two year career with the department, the last fifteen as a detective. Lines were notched in his face from the years of job pressure. He combed back his thin gray hair with his fingers as Martinez entered the room.

"Hello, Frank. I wasn't expecting you, thought they'd give you the day watch this close to retirement."

"Hell, no, they keep me on the graveyard to remind me that I want to get out. With a day job, I might hang around longer. And they wouldn't want that. Besides, I've been on the shit list my whole career, why ruin a perfect run?"

Martinez laughed. "Have you talked to our patient?"

"He sounds more like a suspect. He's still in and out, mostly out. What the hell did you give him?"

"Pain meds that will wear off soon."

"Okay Doc, what have we got?"

Martinez led him over to the x-ray charts. "Medium caliber I'd say, .40 caliber or .38 special."

"Can I take a look?"

"Sure." They went to the ER cubicle where the uniform team maintained sentry. The patient was still in slumber land from the medication. The doctor pulled back the sheet covering the man's body, careful not to disconnect the monitors and tubes. The man was well-muscled and of average height. Martinez slowly and carefully removed the tape from the bandage, which contained a small blood spot that penetrated through the gauze. The wound was round and slightly oblong, and the entrance site was clean.

"There's no tattooing," Morrell said, as he performed an examination of his own. "No abrasion ring, no powder burns. He was shot from at least several feet away, by a handgun, held waist to chest high by the shooter. He was shot by someone from across a room while they were face to face." Morrell paused, then continued. "It's a little early to be sure, but I'd say he was in a gunfight. Probably shot by a right-handed person." He then turned to the doctor, lowered his thick eyebrows and said, "Let me ask you something, Doc."

"Yes?"

He spoke as if he was contemplating the mystery of life. "How can this guy take a slug traveling fourteen-hundred feet per second right in the gut and still be alive? No vital organs damaged, bullet sitting harmless in his rib cage. Yet, the next guy who gets wheeled in here might die from a brain hemorrhage he got from a fall in the bathtub. What is it? Luck of the draw? A fluke? Divine providence?"

"I don't know, Frank," Martinez answered in an undertone, "I've only had three years to wonder about the same thing. You've had three decades and still don't have the answer."

A young plainclothes officer in a threadbare suit joined them, carrying a large black case and a professional thirty-five millimeter Nikon. At Morrell's direction, he took several close-up photos of the entrance wound. Morrell stepped around the female uniformed officer to the head of the bed, and turned the patient's head straight in order to take a facial photograph. "Print him," Morrell commanded. The Crime Lab Technician then opened his black case and removed a blank fingerprint card, an inked pad, and a spoon-like metal device. He inked the patient's fingertips and singularly rolled them onto the card, held in place by the spoon, a method used mostly to fingerprint corpses with non-responsive fingers. "Give that to O'Neil," Morrell told him, "and get me those pictures ASAP. One more thing. Get a paraffin wax kit and let's test for powder burns on his hands."

"Yes, sir."

Morrell turned to the senior sentry. "Stay with him, and have the precinct send someone to book him."

"What do we book him with?" asked the officer.

"I'll think of something."

Lieutenant Larry O'Neil sat hunched over a wide glass-top desk and peered through a magnified lens at two fingerprint cards placed side-by-side on the desk. The rotund, ruddy-faced Irishman, wearing glasses, was one of the premier fingerprint experts in the state, with more than twenty years in the Bureau of Identification. He picked up the card on the left side and placed it on top of a foot- high stack to his left. He removed a new card from a stack on the right side, and compared it to his known sample taken from the suspect in the hospital. He had repeated this procedure for over an hour. This time, he looked back and forth at the two cards several times. He did so again. And again. He saw arches on both left thumbs. Whorls on both left index fingers. Loops on the remaining left hand fingers. Then similar matches on the two sets of right hand prints, including the palm prints that were rolled out on the bottom of the cards. He examined them a final time through his lens, then sat back in his chair and read the name on the file card that perfectly matched his unknown suspect: James J. Bratton. Male Caucasian, age thirty-three. Numerous arrests in New Orleans. Four year stretch in the Louisiana State Penitentiary at Angola.

O'Neil placed the two cards containing identical fingerprints in a clear envelope. He squared the remaining stacks of fingerprint cards on his desk and handed them to a clerk for re-filing. "And get me Sergeant Morrell," he told the clerk.

The following day Morrell returned to the hospital and questioned the suspect, who was now in a private room, still under police guard. "We know who you are, Jimmy,"

Morrell told him in a friendly manner. "Now tell me why you're here."

Bratton inched up in the bed and winced in discomfort. "I'm not telling you shit," he replied in a defiant tone.

"That bullet needs to come out. When it does, we'll know the rest of the story."

"It ain't coming out."

"If not, you'll die." Morrell lied, but Bratton had no way of knowing.

"So what? Let me die."

Morrell's voice changed into a brief, one man good-cop bad-cop routine. He scowled, "It's not that easy, you asshole."

The interview was over. Morrell had Bratton's photograph sent to law enforcement agencies in Louisiana and adjoining states for possible identification in robberies or other shooting incidents. He quickly became a suspect in the robbery at the Commerce Bank and Trust Company of Louisiana and the murder of Officer Bobby Cazale'. New Orleans police detectives had negative results from witness interviews; they could not identify Bratton because the perpetrators had worn stockings over their heads during the robbery. Bratton fit the general physical description of the killer, but that was flimsy at best. A match of the bullet in Bratton's body to Officer Cazale's gun was now critical, and would give them a boilerplate case. Morrell wasted no more time trying to convince Bratton to have surgery. He charged him with being a material witness, which would hold him in the hospital indefinitely. He then sought a court order to have the bullet removed from Bratton's body as evidence.

Withstanding more than a few roadblocks thrown in his path by Bratton's court-appointed attorney, a judicial order was issued two days later allowing doctors to remove the bullet. Morrell scrubbed in, donned a mask and gown, and witnessed the surgeons remove a pristine, striated, .38 special caliber round nose bullet from Bratton's chest cavity, along with a small fragment. Because of the location of the entrance wound, Bratton would have died in the bank lobby if the ammunition had been hollow-point instead of round nose. For a moment, Morrell now questioned whether indeed Bratton was the killer, since the bullet fired into Bratton was a .38 special, and Cazale's service revolver was a .357 caliber. Both calibers could be fired from that weapon, and only ballistics tests could confirm one way or the other. Morrell briefly inspected the bullet in his latex-gloved hand, then turned it over directly to NOPD detectives who immediately transported it to their forensics laboratory. Within hours, the bullet was positively identified as having been fired from Officer Cazale's weapon.

Despite Morrell's marathon sessions with Bratton and his attorney, the killer would make no deals to give further details of the bank robbery, his accomplices, or what happened to the stolen cash and securities. An all points bulletin issued for the Thunderbird that had dumped Bratton at the emergency room failed to produce the vehicle or its driver. The robbery/murder remained an open, high priority case for the New Orleans Police Department as well as the Federal Bureau of Investigation. Sergeant Frank Morrell, the grizzled detective, could hang up his yoke knowing that he solved the cop killer case - at least a part of it.

Assassin Hunter

CHAPTER 1

Pickle Nose Willie gingerly picked up the dice shoved in front of him by Benny the stickman. He held one of the red cellulose cubes between his thumb and middle finger and spun it around, then snatched it into his hand along with its mate and shook them furiously. He threw his fist forward and opened his fingers at the same time, and the dice danced along the green felt table to the opposite side and bounced off the side board, landing face up on a four and a three. "Hah!" he shouted to no one in particular. Benny reached out with his dice rake and retrieved the red squares, and set them in the middle of the table. "This time I bet fifty," Pickle Nose said. He peeled some bills from his fist and threw them down on the felt stretched across the converted pool table. He was a tall man in his early sixties, somewhat slouched over with rounded shoulders. The sides of his bald head was complemented by long white hair slicked back above his ears. His complexion and long, bulbous nose reddened as his excitement grew. He was usually a ten-dollar player but stepped up his bet after already making three passes with the dice. The assortment of characters crowded around the table all placed cash bets on the pass line as Benny shoved the dice back to Pickle Nose. Small stacks of money in different denominations marked the wagers of each player. Nobody dare bet against a hot shooter on a roll like this, except Suitcase Tommy, who religiously bet the wrong way no matter the shooter or the temperature of the dice.

Pickle Nose again picked up the dice and ceremoniously spun one of them between his fingers, then shook both of them and let them fly to the other side of the table. They landed on six and three, and Benny shouted, "Nine is the point," before corralling the dice and returning them to the shooter. Another round of betting ensued as Pickle Nose picked them up and dropped them straight down from his hands and Benny quickly shouted, "No roll! Goddamn it Willie, throw them all the way against the wall or we'll pass them to the next shooter."

"And you'll kiss my ass, Benny. Gimme them little computers." Some of the men standing elbow-to-elbow around the table laughed. Others yelled for Pickle Nose to shut up and shoot.

The room was the cramped upstairs office of a banana import company near the docks in Mobile, Alabama that handled fruit cargo and gulf coast distribution. The game was run after hours by Thomas Ranzino, better known as Suitcase Tommy, a connected gambler from New Orleans, in collusion with the owner of the otherwise legitimate banana company. Ranzino had a lengthy arrest record and several felony convictions for fencing stolen property. He earned his moniker in his younger days by having a briefcase or small suitcase with him as a constant companion, which he used to display his stolen wares. Everyone smoked in the room, and it was so thick that a cloud hung only a couple of feet above the group. A single bare light bulb suspended by its wire from the twelve-foot ceiling swung slightly over the middle of the table. Besides the players and the house dealers who clutched hands full of cash to fade the bets, were standing-room guys waiting for somebody to tap out so they could squeeze into the action.

As Pickle Nose threw the dice again I was rubbed against by Suitcase Tommy, who was jammed in next to me at the table, and I felt the unmistakable outline of a handgun in his side waistband. Almost everyone in the joint, including me, was packing so it wasn't out of the ordinary for him to be armed - except that he was a convicted felon, a member of the Marcello family, and the target of an ATF undercover investigation. "Six!" shouted Benny, who now quickly returned the dice as more cash piled up on the table and the players anticipated another pass from Willie. Ranzino told Benny to give him the dice.

He closely examined them, then turned to me and asked, "Waddaya think, Tony? Pickle Nose hasn't thrown a hot hand since the Great Depression."

"They look okay to me."

The small crowd jeered as Suitcase Tommy said, "Not good enough." He took a small caliper from his pocket, and looked like a science teacher as he measured each die and found them both to be exactly seven hundred and fifty one-thousandths of an inch, perfect cubes. He dumped the dice back onto the table and grunted, "Okay." A slight cheer erupted and Benny raked the dice back to the shooter.

I slowly backed away from the table to make a phone call from a corner of the room to one of the surveillance agents who were strategically placed around the neighborhood. Pickle Nose then pointed the dice at me and said, "Don't miss out on this, Tony, we're making history."

"Can't a guy go take a piss around here?" I yelled back.

He threw the dice and almost immediately Benny hollered, "Nina! Winnah!" A shout went up from the crowd and the dealers threw more money onto the stacks, which were snapped up by the men tightly packed around the table. Betting reached a frenzy, and while everyone's attention was on the game I quietly went to a phone that sat on a plain metal desk and dialed out.

The lead surveillance agent answered and I whispered, "Tommy's holding. Move whenever you're ready." I shoved my way back to the front of the table in time to place a bet before Pickle Nose came out with the dice again. His point was six, but on the next roll he sevened out. A low, dejected grumble came from the crowd. They had just witnessed a twenty-five minute dice hand, a rarity in the gambling world, yet scoffed at Pickle Nose Willie as if he lost them money. This was a strange, greedy bunch indeed. Like the others, I counted my money after each bet as if somebody was going to take it away from me. I had run up a total of eighteen hundred dollars, not bad considering that Uncle Sam had given me only two hundred to stake the game.

I had participated in the illegal game every Saturday night and most Tuesdays for six months, gathering intelligence on a host of suspects that frequented the place. Every type of miscreant – mob guys, burglars, safe crackers, drug dealers, addicts, pimps, bikers, Neo-Nazis, pickpockets, bookmakers, Ku Klux Klan sympathizers, and career criminals - from New Orleans to Panama City floated in and out of the game. There were also tough but legitimate longshoremen, cab drivers, gamblers, and merchant seamen in the mix, many of whom routinely showed up after the last night race at the nearby greyhound dog track.

After the next shooter failed to make his point with the dice, many of the men backed away from the table. They didn't want to lose the small fortunes luck had brought them after the dice cooled off. It was four o'clock in the morning and the game was ready to break up. I wondered where the troops were, why they hadn't arrived yet. Suitcase Tommy Ranzino would be leaving in a matter of minutes. He instructed his dealers to close shop and stood counting his cash, which he folded into his pocket. He had an olive complexion with a heavy beard, and looked several years older than his true age of forty-five. He bore a thick cut scar on the left side of his neck, which added a sinister look to his always-serious countenance. The players milled around counting their money and congratulated themselves on catching Pickle Nose Willie's hot hand. A muffled rumbling from the stairway leading to the office grew louder, until it sounded like a herd of buffalo wearing shoes was coming up the stairs. Then a single loud crash took down the door, which was bolted and chained. Within a second, four men, in blue fatigues adorned with ATF AGENT in gold lettering, were standing in the room holding a large iron battering ram. In another second the room was filled with agents, their guns drawn, shouting, "Federal agents with a search warrant."

Several of the men scrambled to a side entrance, only to find it blocked by agents. A few tried to inconspicuously rid themselves of the guns and knives they had hidden in their clothing. Suitcase Tommy sidled next to me and I felt his hand inside my jacket pocket. He winked at me as he let go of his gun, and I felt its weight tug at my clothes. Unwittingly, he had just ditched his weapon to an undercover ATF agent.

Along with the other characters in the game, I was made to assume the position spread eagle against a wall and searched. At least a dozen of the men were wanted for various crimes, or like Ranzino, for being convicted felons in possession of firearms. The others were released after being checked out by the vice cops who were brought along by ATF to handle the local gambling charges. The two young agents who searched me found Ranzino's .32 caliber automatic in my jacket as well as my .38 special caliber snub-nose revolver, which was stuck in the waistband under my shirt. They checked the driver's license in my wallet, which identified me as Anthony Parrino. In a matter of minutes their background check on me turned up a conviction for burglary. One of them seemed to be the senior of the team and asked all the questions. I co-operated as least I could, which landed me in handcuffs so tight that my fingers turned blue. None of the agents knew me except the one in charge, who purposely ignored me. I attracted special attention since I was the only one found with two guns. My wrists were in pain as they placed me in a G-car with Suitcase Tommy and transported us to the federal holding facility at the county jail.

During the booking process I glanced all around for the agent in charge, to no avail. He was supposed to have me released from jail under the guise of posting bond after everyone had been booked, but he never showed. Because the arrest was made early Sunday morning, I was held in jail until those of us who didn't post bond were brought before the U.S. Magistrate the next morning. I had been in worse jails working undercover, but spending that next thirty-six hours in the lockup wasn't exactly a pleasant experience, and wasn't supposed to happen.

Two deputy U.S. Marshals picked me up Monday morning and brought me into court for arraignment. When my case was called, an assistant United States attorney fresh out of law school stood up and read the charges against me. "Anthony Parrino, convicted felon in possession of a firearm." The judge asked if the arresting agent was present. The prosecutor looked around the courtroom and said in a meek manner, "I don't think so, your honor."

"Is there an arresting agent from the Bureau of Alcohol, Tobacco and Firearms present?" the judge boomed.

Just then, the ATF agent who severely handcuffed me came into the courtroom accompanied by the agent in charge. They both approached the prosecutor and huddled with him. While they spoke, the lawyer kept turning to look at me as if I was a circus freak of some kind, then he finally nodded to the deputy marshal to release me. He approached the bench to explain to the judge. As soon as I was released I walked out into the hallway to the men's room, followed by the agents. We searched the room without speaking to make sure no one else was in there, and the young agent instinctively propped his foot against the door to keep anyone from entering. I couldn't control myself another minute. "What the fuck is going on?" I yelled at the veteran.

"Look, Tony, I'm sorry."

"Sorry? Where the hell were you at booking?"

"There was a mix-up. Confusion. I thought you were sprung."

"My ass. Because of you I had to spend the weekend in the tank with puking drunks and some guy with green teeth who never shut up."

The agent was around forty, and surely had been involved in many of these cases. His dark eyebrows raised apologetically as he stammered out an explanation. "We found out you were still in jail when you didn't show up at the office this morning."

"I don't mind being locked up when there's a reason. But right now I'm a day overdue from contacting my wife in Miami and she's probably going nuts. Understand?"

"Completely. Again, I'm sorry. We've accomplished our mission on this case and we're shutting it down." He hesitated for a moment, then continued, " I've got a message for you. You are to report for a Secret Service detail in Arizona. Tomorrow."

"Well, isn't that great, I won't be home for thirty *more* days."

He sheepishly handed me the orders, which directed me to be in Phoenix. We stared at each other for a moment, then I extended my hand to shake. Relieved at the gesture, he smiled and gripped my hand tightly. The young agent stepped away from the door and out of my way. As I exited, I pointed at him and said to the senior agent, "Show him how to properly handcuff a prisoner."

CHAPTER 2

The aging prop-job creaked and jammed its way to the ground at LaGuardia airport. The afternoon was cold, and the sky was as clear as it gets in New York. I peered out the window at the Manhattan skyline from the World War Two vintage airplane. It was hard to believe that a presidential candidate couldn't, or wouldn't, afford better transportation during the campaign. U.S. Congressman Morris Udall of Arizona was among more than a dozen Democrats taking a shot at the 1975 nomination. He had reached the shaky ground in the campaign where he would either raise enough money for a sustained run, or fizzle with the *also-rans*.

It was the seventeenth day of my thirty-day detail on Secret Service protection, and far enough into the assignment that the days and places began to blur. Plane hopping to five or six cities every day had taken its toll on the Treasury agents, as well as the campaign staff and press corps who were forced companions aboard the ancient aircraft. The only other protection detail that rivaled the bare-bones campaign of Udall up to that point was that of Jimmy Carter, the peanut farmer ex-governor of Georgia. His staff passed out small bags of peanuts at every whistle stop and Democratic caucus meeting. After the meetings many in the crowd would leave the little bags behind on their chairs or on the floor, and his campaign staff retrieved them for redistribution at the next stop.

Mo Udall was a tall, strikingly physical man with one eye who had briefly played professional basketball with the old Denver Nuggets. His sense of humor was legendary. Whenever things got boring during the tedious travel, he threatened to take out his glass eye to amuse the reporters. His political expertise was demonstrated by his repetitious speeches and canned answers in jousting with the press. He favored gun control legislation, but in keeping with the political art of reaching out to the masses, whenever he was questioned about the subject he always began his answer by saying, "Let me first state that I represent the old Tombstone Territory in congress." This conjured up thoughts of the old west when everyone carried firearms. In short order, the nature of protecting Udall's life had forced me to listen to his rhetoric over and over again at each campaign stop, to the point that I could have given the speeches myself, verbatim.

He often opened his speeches with a joke, and told his audience how, during the New Hampshire primary, he walked into a barber shop and announced that he was running for president. The barber replied, "We were just laughing about that this morning." Udall was well-liked on both sides of the congressional aisle and eventually served thirty years in Washington.

Each time the old plane revved up its propellers or landed I couldn't help drawing a comparison to the sleek, shiny 727 the detail had traveled on several months earlier which transported former California governor Ronald Reagan across the country. He became the only serious challenger to the incumbent Republican, Gerald Ford, and his campaign set the stage for his eventual election to the White House four years later. The Gipper traveled in style and the trappings of his campaign belied the fact that in the end, he would be the *also-ran* for the Republican nomination while his counterpart, Jimmy Carter, swept his party's nomination, and eventually the presidency, in a groundswell of popularity. The Secret Service was stretched out farther than ever before in history during this presidential election for two major reasons.

First, a large number of Democrats sensed a political kill on President Gerald Ford, the Vice-President who was elevated to the office by default when Richard Nixon resigned amidst the Watergate scandal. Congressmen Morris Udall of Arizona and Lloyd Bentsen of Texas, United States senators Hubert Humphrey of Minnesota, Henry "Scoop" Jackson of Washington, and Frank Church of Idaho all had campaigns cranked up, as well as former senator George McGovern. They all had correctly smelled blood and each wanted to be the Democrat to take advantage of the vulnerable president who had not been elected to his office. In addition, former senator Eugene McCarthy, California governor Jerry Brown, and Alabama governor George Wallace, who had been cut down and paralyzed by gunfire while campaigning for the Democratic nomination in 1972, were all running campaigns as independents. Indeed, it was the assassination attempt on Wallace in a Maryland shopping center parking lot that nudged congress into expanding the protection responsibilities of the Treasury Department to include major presidential candidates.

Second, the manpower shortage was heightened by the fact that 1976 was the Bicentennial of the country. There were many celebrations and tributes paid by foreign dignitaries and heads of state, all of which received Secret Service protection while on American soil. The protection details, especially in New York because of its location of the United Nations, often ran over and into each other's radio transmissions due to the large number of personnel involved. Agents from various assignments literally bumped into each other. To make matters worse and more complicated, there were protection details from the State Department whose agents handled security for the U.S. Ambassadors to overseas countries who returned for the Bicentennial functions. At times it seemed like half the city of New York was populated by gun-carrying agents or their protectees. By having ATF, U.S. Customs, and IRS special agents assigned to the unprecedented number of Secret Service details, the Treasury Department's law enforcement agencies were stretched to the breaking point while struggling to maintain their daily investigative missions.

The long and irregular hours, lack of days off, extensive travel, and the rigors and intensity of protection work took its toll on all of us. Normally, gripes from agents were summarily dismissed by the detail leader, who was always a supervisory agent of the Secret Service. But on Udall's detail that happened to be Ernie Chinn, a classmate of mine just a few years earlier at the U.S. Treasury Law Enforcement Academy in Washington, D.C. Ernie was a Chinese-American from the west coast who, on rare days off during Treasury basic training, had given me surfing lessons at Ocean City, Maryland. We were both ex-cops from big cities which made us kindred spirits apart from the Phi Beta Kappa's with newly-minted college diplomas hired by the Powers That Be in the Treasury Department to be molded into Treasury's desired image. We also shared an affinity for 50's music and on nights off we had gone to a little bar in Frederick, Maryland to participate in the trivia contest. The band would play a number and the first to name it and the original artist was awarded a magnum of champagne. After several visits there, the manager gave us the bubbly as soon as we walked in and asked us to keep quiet during the contest.

Ernie had a wild sense of humor and called me "Muss," which was short for Mussolini. His good-hearted dig at my Italian heritage had originated from my constant complaints about scheduling on the detail. He made an analogy to Benito Mussolini's promise during his dictatorship to make the trains in Italy run on time. After we completed basic training, Ernie and I went separate ways and began careers with our respective agencies, but we kept in touch and remained under the same Treasury enforcement umbrella. I hadn't seen him since the Washington days until I showed up for the Udall detail and found that he was my boss.

"Hey, Ernie, why don't you call D.C. and tell them this plane is a flying piece of crap and we shouldn't be on it," I snorted to him as we stood up to stretch while the plane taxied to the terminal.

One of the press reporters also stretching in the aisle looked Ernie right in the eye while pointing a finger toward me and said, "I'm with him."

As we descended the steps to the tarmac, a young agent approached with a written message. Ernie read it and turned his foppish, blue-black hair toward me and with a sarcastic grin punctuated by ultra-white teeth he snarled, "Okay Muss, you got your wish about not flying on this plane. Looks like you're off the detail." I waited for some sign that it was a joke, but he shoved the note in my fist.

"They want you to call Washington from a pay phone. Call me at the hotel when you find out what's up."

Several things flashed through my mind, not the least of which was that I wouldn't again have to board that poor excuse for a flying machine. I surveyed the note and recognized the phone number as an ATF Headquarters exchange. I wondered what was in store and what the importance was of pulling me out in the middle of a protection detail. But foremost was the anticipation that I would soon be home with my wife and one-year-old, first-born child, a bright, wiry boy whose personality duplicated mine.

The protection details during this election year were assigned for thirty days at a time, alternating thirty days at my assigned ATF district office performing the varied and demanding "routine" duties. Criminals of all descriptions run afoul of the laws enforced by ATF and the agency is in daily combat with a variety of dangerous individuals and groups. ATF's mission is far-reaching and the demands on physical and mental agility are great, as evidenced by the fact that ATF has had more agents killed in the line of duty than any other federal agency. Despite my puzzlement at being yanked from the detail, I was indeed looking forward to what I thought was the rotation back home.

CHAPTER 3

I called the ATF Headquarters number from a pay phone in the lobby at LaGuardia. A female voice answered in a most businesslike manner, "Covert operations." I wasn't expecting to reach the sneaky squad.

"This is Special Agent Palumbo from the Miami office. I'm on protection detail in New York and just received a message to call."

"Just a moment."

While I was on hold I tried to figure out what they wanted with me. Did something go wrong on the Suitcase Tommy Ranzino case? The receiver clicked and my musing was interrupted. "Hello, Tony, this is Phil McKinney. How's it going?"

"Okay I guess, except I'm punch drunk from travel. This morning I had to look at the phone book in my hotel to find out where I was. How about you? I haven't seen you in some time."

"As well as can be expected. I've kept track of your undercover work. We have one we think you'll fit perfectly and it has to be moved on right away. It's being run out of New Orleans. I'd like you to come here for a briefing before you return to Miami. We've already checked the flight schedules and you can be here by eight-thirty." I knew better than to talk about it on the phone, so I exchanged pleasantries with McKinney and hung up. It was now early evening and my flight to Washington didn't allow time to go to the hotel in Manhattan. I waited long enough for the detail to arrive at their quarters, then called Ernie Chinn at the Loew's Summit on Lexington and Fifty-first.

I gave the hotel operator Ernie's code name and was plugged into his room. "No more freezing my ass off with you guys. I'm on my way to D.C. tonight. Can you have my things forwarded to Miami?"

"You got it, Muss, you lucky bastard. Now I'm short again on the detail. You owe me."

"Try to collect."

"Up yours."

I didn't give Ernie any indication what this was all about, but he was seasoned enough to know it wasn't routine. He also knew the significance of losing a man off the detail during the critical manpower shortage. As he got off the phone he instinctively said, "Hey, Muss, take care and tell Gina hello for me . . . and wherever you're going, be sure to cover your ass."

The flight to Washington was a welcome respite from the daily travel intensity of the detail. Because of the short booking notice the only seats available were in first class and I enjoyed the amenities. For the next hour I truly relaxed physically for the first time in several weeks. The horizon darkened outside the window and I thought of my family at home. They didn't have a clue where I was or where I was going. I made a mental note to call Gina when I arrived in Washington. I turned out the overhead light and placed my head against the backseat, which vibrated from the plane's engines. I had become accustomed to falling asleep in that position.

I thought about how much time I had been away from home in the first year of my son's life and that I hadn't planned it that way. I had wanted children for several years but Gina resisted, wanting first to complete her college degree and later to attend graduate school. Although her mother was Italian – Sicilian, moreover – she considered herself somewhat liberated from the traditional views about having children right away and wanted to put off the demands of parenting until she was educated and ready for the challenge. Even my own relentless desire to have kids was tempered by the fact that all around me were agents who were living testimonials to the broken homes caused by a job that cared little for anything except its mission. When we agreed to have Nick I was ecstatic and pledged to be the best father I could.

The flight attendant appeared with the drink cart and I instinctively waved her away, then suddenly sat up and ordered vodka. I sipped the clear liquid slowly, and enjoyed the burning sensation that passed across my lips and down my throat. The relatively odorless drink wouldn't leave a smell on my breath but might relieve some tension. I wasn't much of a drinker but had acquired a taste for vodka by frequenting bars and nightclubs working undercover. The shot relaxed me even more and I dozed off for several minutes. I was awakened by the *dong dong dong* of the signal that we were making the approach to Dulles International. I shook out the cobwebs and concentrated on the meeting ahead. I usually took all assignments in stride, but apprehension began to build because of the way this was handled.

In the airport lobby I called home, but there was no answer. I jumped into a taxi and headed to ATF Headquarters in the Treasury Department building. The cabbie's radio blared continuous coverage about the Super Bowl to be played in Miami that weekend. I walked past the statue of Alexander Hamilton and up the steps to the night entrance of the impressive, staid old building near the White House, and recalled the hours of target practice spent in the basement there on Saturday mornings while attending Special Agent basic training. I flashed my I.D. folder and badge to the guard and signed into his logbook. I walked down the old marble corridor past the glass doorways of the offices, most of which were dark. My pace quickened as I approached the Covert Operations office where the lights were on and there was office activity.

Jim Fenton greeted me. He was a jovial law school grad I had worked with several times before. He was a constitutional law scholar and taught the block of courses on search and seizure in the ATF Academy. We had worked together teaching a series of training schools for local and state police officers conducted by ATF and funded by the Justice Department. I was tapped to instruct on the history and modus operandi of the mafia and other organized crime groups. Our dog-and-pony show had taken us to many cities, and I particularly enjoyed working with him.

"Jim, are you working here now?"

"Don't curse me like that," he grinned as we shook hands firmly. "They called me into this for a little legal advice, and I'm the guy who knows as little as anybody." He hadn't disappointed by greeting me with a joke and we both laughed. I felt more comfortable chatting with him for a few minutes. He had reached the mandatory retirement age for federal law enforcement of fifty-five, but had been granted extensions because of his expertise. He began his career chasing bootleggers in Brooklyn, and eventually became the top legal mind in ATF. He refused many times to become the agency's general counsel in favor of remaining a Special Agent. Although he was part of the Headquarters staff, we had often bitched to each other about the stumbling blocks the bureaucracy placed in the path of the agents working the streets.

We were joined by Phil McKinney and one of his assistants, an agent with extensive undercover experience. The undone neckties, rolled-up sleeves, and facial stubble on these men removed some of my self-consciousness about being unable to shave or change clothes. This was a group accustomed to working long hours under pressure, and they looked the part. McKinney was a blue-eyed, blonde son of the South who had worked undercover so deep and so long infiltrating the Ku Klux Klan that his children were born in his undercover name. He had to have their names legally changed back to McKinney when he was pulled out from under. He was a dedicated agent who rose through the ranks to head Covert Operations and would eventually become a deputy director of the agency. His office monitored all the major cases and ran the undercover pool. He wasted no time.

"Tony, I'll give you the situation straight. One of our informants has advised us through the New Orleans office that a contract murder is about to go down in the Cajun country of southwest Louisiana. A suspect is approaching local thugs, trying to hire a mafia hit man from New Orleans. The guy is serious. He's been flashing wads of money to show he's not playing around. We need you to take that contract before some real killers do."

"What is ATF's jurisdiction here?" I asked. "Murder isn't a federal crime."

"That's why we called Jim into this. He thinks we're on firm legal ground not referring this to the local police."

Jim Fenton took a long puff from his ever-present pipe, and exhaled a large billow as he laid the pipe down into a large opaque ashtray. "The suspect is offering to supply the murder weapon, some type of firearm including a silencer, which is clearly ATF jurisdiction. In addition, even if we aren't successful in intercepting the murder contract, and he does reach a mob guy, chances are the assassin will be a convicted felon and we can bust him for possessing a firearm. And of course, we can add conspiracy charges to both of them and anybody else you find involved."

"There's more," McKinney added. "We have a problem with corruption in the Louisiana parish where the suspect lives. If we turn this case over to the locals they won't do shit, so that's not an option. If they get word it could be more dangerous for you. We also don't know the identity of the intended victim or victims, or their location, and we don't know whether or not somebody in the Marcello mob has already been hired. Your job is to get the murder contract and connect the dots before a body turns up. Everybody involved in this, including the informant, is involved with racehorses. You've got a racetrack background."

"As a general rule mob guys don't kill for money," I pointed out. "Murder is used as an enforcement tool within their world but it's rarely commercialized. In fact, taking murder contracts outside of family business is forbidden."

McKinney shot back, "We know all this. But we can't afford to blow this thing off. There's too many cowboys out there, fringe mob associates who would love to make a nice money score and share it with the bosses. Depending on how this thing pans out, Carlos Marcello or one of his lieutenants might be brought into it." We sat quiet for a minute, mulling over each other's comments. McKinney broke the silence. "We don't know where this thing is going, but we have to move *now*. There's at least one life on the line and we don't know whose. As always, you have the right to refuse this assignment with no repercussions and no questions asked."

I looked back and forth at Fenton and McKinney. I knew I had been selected from the undercover pool that uses the time-honored method of matching the agent to an assignment by analyzing his or her background, education, and life experience. A pale-faced Irishman would stick out in the scores of Little Italy's around the country, as well as in this case. A young agent right out of college wouldn't fit in working the gritty docks of the port cities. It wasn't necessary for McKinney to go into his reasons for plucking me from the undercover pool, a data base of dozens of agents specially trained and suited for this type operation. All my grandparents were born in Sicily. I was born and raised in New Orleans, had been a police officer there and knew many of the street characters and how they operated. I knew enough about organized crime that ATF had me teach new agents about it. Perhaps most important, I had undercover experience and a good success rate. Being from Louisiana, I was familiar with the Cajuns from the bayous and swamplands in the part of the state near Lafayette. They couldn't *order* me into this, but I knew how much had gone into their selection process.

"Who is my contact agent?"

McKinney now sat up straight and his eyes widened. My question confirmed that I would take the assignment, and he knew his selection phase was complete. "Your contact agent is Lyle Melancon. His background and knowledge of the Acadian culture will help. He's fluent in Cajun French. Get in touch with him first thing in the morning and plan to be in New Orleans as soon as possible. We'll monitor the case through the Special Agent in Charge of the New Orleans office. The SAC there is Jim King, a good man. We worked together in the old major violator program. We'll provide any support you need. Any questions?"

"How long do I have at home before reporting?"

"The weekend. That's it. Be in New Orleans Monday morning. Good hunting."

McKinney and his assistant retreated back to his office. Fenton and I remained talking for several minutes. He told me a few anecdotes about the happenings at Headquarters, which made me laugh. As we shook hands to part, I mockingly chastised him, "Never trust the Supreme Court of the United States." He used that admonishment to his students each time he lectured on cases in which the court reversed its own previous ruling.

I opted to take the redeye flight home instead of spending the night in Washington, in order to maximize my time at home before Monday. I taxied back to the airport, and the cab's radio was full of the same Super Bowl coverage I had heard on the way over. I booked the first flight to Miami, then phoned home. Gina answered in a sleepy voice. I hadn't realized it was almost midnight.

"Hey, babe," I growled in a low tone. "How are you guys?"

"Fine, Tony. Are you okay? What time is it?"

"Sure, I'm okay. Sorry to call so late, but I've got good news. I'll be home in a few hours. I won't wake you."

"That's great! Nick will be so excited. I love you."

"Me too. Sleep well."

It was great to hear her voice, and I smiled at the thought of being with her. But the smile faded when I boarded the plane and thought about having to explain to her that my time at home would be all so brief.

CHAPTER 4

I deplaned in Miami at four-thirty in the morning. The airport was jammed with people wearing funny hats and clothes of all descriptions. Their color combinations were the blue and silver of the Dallas Cowboys or the black and gold of the Pittsburgh Steelers. They had made the pilgrimage to Super Bowl X to cheer their respective teams and were huddled in groups, large and small, at the various restaurants and bars in the terminal building. I braced myself for the task of trying to get ground transportation in the middle of all the party-goers. I approached the cab stands where the line was a block long. Before frustration set in, I spotted Iggy Morales, a U.S. Customs agent I had worked with in the area, standing beside a baggage checkpoint.

"Hi, Tony. You look like hell. Where are you coming from?"

"You name it, I'm coming from there."

"You'll never get a cab with all this craziness going on. I'm leaving this crappy airport detail in a few minutes if you'd like a lift."

"Are you kidding?" His words were quite welcome. We got into his government car and drove through a small throng of confused but happy fans as they tried to figure out how they were getting to their hotels. Iggy was short in stature, with dark hair and eyes, and spoke with a slight Hispanic accent. He was talkative during the ride. He told me he had only been back in town for a couple of weeks, having returned from the protection detail of Senator Hubert Humphrey. "How do you like that guy?" he asked, although he didn't wait for an answer. "He was already the Vice-President of the United States under Lyndon Johnson, loses out when Nixon gets the White House, gets himself elected to the U.S. Senate for the second time, and now he wants to be the fucking president! Some guys just never have enough."

"Iggy, I think you and I are the only two guys left in the country who aren't running for president." We laughed out loud. I told him I was returning from Mo Udall's detail. "We should get up a betting pool on the order that each of the candidates drops out of the process."

"Well, at least now you'll be home for a month."

"Yeah, I'm looking forward to it." That was true, but confirming that I'd be home for a month was a lie. Lies to protect undercover roles had now become second nature to me. I could have explained to him that my visit home was a short one, and that I would be moving right on to another assignment, but it wasn't worth the effort. The lie would do. Living and telling lies is the essence of undercover work and I had learned to be good at it and do it whenever it suited the purpose. We talked about the candidates and their sometimes hilarious efforts to get the high ground in the campaign. We cruised past countless palm trees and were soon at my front door. I thanked Iggy and he drove off in the G-car. My baggage was still back in New York, and the only thing I carried was my overcoat, hardly needed in the sub-tropic locale, even in January.

I fumbled with my keys and didn't easily remember which one fit the bolt lock that I had installed myself when Nick was born. I quietly walked to the bedroom and looked at Gina, who was sound asleep. I rested my eyes on her and enjoyed the calming effect. Nick was in his room sleeping on his stomach. I patted his back gently and enjoyed the touch of his warm little body and the fine hair on his head. I stuck a finger inside the waist of his diaper. It was wet so I changed him into a dry one without waking him. I thought about how many diaper changes he had without me in the past year. I wondered how many new words he had bleated out without my hearing them. I patted him once again, then made my way to our bedroom where I threw my clothes to the floor and crawled in bed with Gina, then wrapped my arms around her. Before I could deliver even one kiss, I fell asleep.

The next morning I awoke to slapping and pounding to the side of my face and neck. I raised my arms to deflect the violent blows. In a flash I recalled my training on how to protect the body and vital organs by covering up until the senses were regained during an attack. As my head cleared, I heard the falsetto chuckles of a child, my child, then the "Dad-dy! Dad-dy!" chorus repeating. Nick had come into my room on his own and decided that I had enough sleep. I lay there and kept my eyes closed as he continued to strike me with his little arms. I pretended to be asleep, then suddenly peeled open one eye and stared at him with it. He stood beside the bed and our eyes were now only inches apart. He paused, then let out a shriek as I jumped up and grabbed him by surprise.

Gina came running into the room and snatched him out of my arms. She couldn't control the anger in her voice. "Damn you, Tony. You're gone all the time and now that you're home you frighten him." She had said so much. I was gone all the time, and when I did return home I felt like a stranger in many ways. I had no knowledge of the everyday happenings in the household. I didn't know who Nick played with and where, nor his new likes and dislikes since I last spent much time with him. It tugged on me to think about it.

"I was just playing, babe. I'm sorry."

Except for this incident, things were upbeat at home for the rest of the weekend. We spent all the time together except when I caught a few minutes of the Super Bowl on television. I decided not to tell Gina about the new assignment until the weekend was over, although she knew something was up since I was home in the middle of the thirty-day protection detail. We enjoyed the time tremendously, and Sunday night, after I rocked Nick to sleep in an old rocking chair, I told Gina I was leaving for New Orleans the next morning. She had taken each of these frequent partings a little harder than the previous one. Tears welled up in her eyes. "How long?" she whispered.

"Don't know." The next words were the hardest to get out. "It's an undercover assignment, could be a couple of weeks or a few months."

She came to life quickly. "Only a few Goddamned months? You just came off one of those six month assignments a couple weeks ago and went straight to a Secret Service detail. Now you're going on another extended one? How many damn agents does ATF have? Why are *you* going again?"

I told her as much as I thought I could, that it would be near New Orleans, although I'd actually be a couple hundred miles from the city. She took solace in the fact that I had friends in the New Orleans office, and figured they would somehow look after me a little better than if I was someplace else. I dried her tears and we made love, then fell asleep in each other's arms.

Assassin Hunter

CHAPTER 5

The next morning a rookie agent picked me up at New Orleans International airport. He had no clue why I was there or any knowledge of the case, and transported me to the SAC office. Special Agent in Charge Jim King and Lyle Melancon, my contact agent, were waiting for me. King had coffee brought in and quickly established himself as an easygoing administrator. Hidden beneath his mild manner was years of experience in undercover work. Like Phil McKinney, King had worked undercover for such long periods of time that his children were born in his undercover surname. He was neatly dressed in a dark brown suit and his highly polished shoes drew attention to his overall neat appearance. He was in his late forties and had salt-and-pepper hair combed over a wide forehead. He wore half-sized reading glasses low on the end of his nose and often peered above them when he spoke.

"Lyle is one of our best men, Tony. He's suited for this case and I wouldn't give you anybody less to work with. He knows the bayous and its people. He also knows your background and has met with the confidential informant."

Lyle was a bear of a man, not so much in height but in density and strength. His crystal blue eyes softened the lines in his face that indicated his veteran status. He had served with several federal agencies and was a journeyman in ATF. "The CI is scared shitless." Lyle's voice had a trace of the Cajun French accent I had heard many times before. "He played with this thing for a while, but when he realized he had knowledge of a serious murder plot that might involve the mafia, he got scared and dimed to us. He's strictly a lightweight in the overall scheme of things as far as criminal activity down there. But, we need him to set you in to a nightclub where lots of shit goes down."

"Any chance this guy is playing two ends to the middle?" I wanted to know as much about this informant as possible, since my life might depend on him.

"At this point, who knows? You're gonna need eyes in the back of your head for this tricky thing." His tone and attitude told me he had lots of experience dealing with confidential informants. He didn't vouch for the guy because he wasn't Lyle's informant, but had been turned over to Lyle by another agent.

"Has this CI been reliable in the past?"

"He's been in our files for a couple of years. We took him down on a gun charge some time back, and developed him as a snitch when he rolled over on his partners in a scheme to transport cheap firearms into Louisiana from Texas. He's given us a couple of hard cases but we use him mostly to take the temperature in Acadiana, intelligence gathering."

Jim King stood up and said, "God knows we wouldn't be in business without informants, especially the undercover business. But they're all slimy bastards." Then he looked me in the eye to let me know what was important from his end. "The guys in the ivory tower are monitoring this closely. Do what you need to do. But be damned sure to keep me apprised of anything that can blow up on us." King's intercom buzzed. "Okay guys, that must be some high potentate on the phone to make my life miserable. I'm sure Lyle has your logistics covered. If you gentlemen don't need anything further of me I'll take this call and get back to my paper shuffling. Good hunting."

After the meeting broke up Lyle took me to the firearms and evidence vault, a large room secured with heavy cage wire that was filled with weapons of all types. We walked past defused bombs, mortars and shells, bazookas, and rocket launchers seized from criminals and being held as evidence. We walked through the cage door where the machine guns, silencers, and clandestine weapons were kept. The vault was somber and silent, empty of people and a stark reminder of the large numbers of the tools of death intercepted by ATF. My standard issue firearm was a Smith & Wesson .357 magnum revolver, hardly suitable for undercover work, and particularly not in this case. I couldn't easily conceal this bulky, heavy, shiny metal handgun, and it isn't the type usually carried by street criminals on their person. And of course, the ATF badge stamped on the firearm was a dead giveaway.

We looked through the large collection of guns and I selected a Smith & Wesson .38 special caliber snub-nosed, the type I usually used for easy concealment. Even though these guns were usually kept in pristine condition, I told Lyle I wanted to test fire it myself. We went to a small indoor range in the office that was used mostly for test firing confiscated weapons, but good enough for my immediate purpose. I loaded the revolver with five rounds from a new box of fifty, and put the remaining rounds in my attaché case. As Lyle watched I fired the five rounds in rapid succession at a target and emptied the chamber in a little more than a second. The black of the bull's eye was gone.

"Hey, boy, where did you learn to shoot like that?" Lyle had a serious look on his face.

"From my mafia relatives."

He laughed, but knew that besides the extensive ATF training, I had been a police officer. Then his face got even more serious. "I've got a special assignment of my own for you."

"What's that?"

"I can nail a wild rabbit at fifty yards with a shotgun, been hunting all my life. But I can't hit the broad side of a barn with a handgun. When our firearms qualifying comes up twice a year I stress out. Last time they kept me on the range for three days before I made it, and threatened to redline me. Hell, Tony, I'll be stuck behind a desk if I don't make it. Your assignment is get me qualified before I have a heart attack over this shit. The range officer is here tomorrow, it's our qualification day."

"Tell you what. I'll qualify along with your office tomorrow. Just be sure to get the position next to me on the range and I'll get you qualified."

The following day Lyle drove us to a remote area of east New Orleans where we met with the range officer and about thirty special agents. These were all veterans who had been through the routine of qualifying many times. They all had to maintain the high priority of firearms proficiency by qualifying the ATF course twice a year. Lyle made sure he was in the same wave of shooters with me as we took our firing positions. He took the position next to me. "Now what, Tony?"

"Now nothing. You just fire the course and do your best. Let me worry about it. You'll qualify." He was puzzled, but he turned to face his old nemesis, the familiar black silhouette of a man reaching to his side as if to draw a gun. As we fired the hundreds of rounds at the targets spaced out at different intervals, I concentrated on firing the best I could, assuring as many bull's eyes as possible on my target. Then, I fired every tenth shot into Lyle's target, which was next to mine up range. When we got past fifty yards to the target, I fired a couple of additional rounds into his blackened concentric circles. My shots onto his target scored, and compensated for the shots he threw completely off. When the range officer announced the scores, he couldn't hold back.

"Holy shit, Melancon. You scored eighty on the first round. Wonders never cease." He continued calling out the scores, and mine was in the eighties instead of the high nineties, still more than enough to qualify. Nobody knew what happened, including Lyle. When the scores were read, he got an excited but dumb look on his face. He looked at me with the same puzzled expression on his mug that he had before we started. But he remained cool and didn't say a word. We packed up our gear and got back in his G-car. He couldn't wait to start talking.

"I've been around the world twice and seen everything three times, but nothing like that. What in hell happened? Did I get better just standing next to you?"

"You know what happened. Just help me get done with this case before we have to come back and do it again in six months." He handed me his meaty paw and shook my hand.

"You're aces in my book, *paisan*."

The firing range incident began a bonding process that was important to us both. I learned that he was a career agent dedicated to the profession and wasn't just going through the motions on the job. Lyle found that I could be trusted, would bend the rules and wouldn't trash his career for the sake of my own if things went sour. He would be my lifeline to the outside world, my only contact with reality once I was submerged in the case. I would have to put my complete trust and faith in him in many ways. I had now established myself with him as a standup guy worthy of his best effort.

It approached dark and the G-car wound through the streets of the Crescent City to a large gated parking lot. There were many different vehicles stored there, mostly seized by ATF for transporting illegal firearms and forfeited to the government for its use. I looked past the Ford Crown Victorias and Chevrolet Caprices that looked like poorly-disguised squad cars. I declined a beautiful Lincoln Continental as being too flashy, as well as the ostentatious Cadillacs and Mercedes-Benzes that would raise eyebrows in Cajun country. The big cars might raise questions about why a professional killer, a paid assassin, would draw attention to himself with such a vehicle. I picked out a late model midnight-blue Camaro, and although it was winter I made sure the air conditioner worked well, knowing the case might drag on into the warm months that begin early in the deep South. Lyle climbed in the car with me and I quickly tested the V-8 engine's acceleration from a dead stop. I hit the freeway and opened her up. "Hell, Tony, we'll never make retirement like this."

We drove around the city and Lyle spent the rest of the night giving me a tutorial, a lay of the land and cultural background of the people inhabiting the twenty-two Louisiana parishes known as Acadiana. We stopped in at the Napoleon House, a popular French Quarter bar he seemed to be familiar with. We relaxed and he gave me a history lesson. "The French fled their homeland in the 1700's seeking religious freedom in far away Nova Scotia, then fled there because of British persecution, and finally landed in the swamps and bayous of southwest Louisiana. They found the area conducive to their trades as hunters and trappers, fishermen and shrimpers, and enjoyed the freedoms they sought. They lived close to the land and waterways and preserved a distinct culture and language different from any other in the United States, one that still flourishes."

I already knew that the Cajuns were a gregarious clan and that they enjoy the simple things in life like cooking and music, for which they are now famous. But Lyle drilled home a side of the Cajun culture I would soon see for myself. He continued, "Cajuns are frugal, a trait inherited form two-hundred years of fending for themselves, and yet they have a great penchant for gambling. They are clannish in some of their customs, to the point of being secretive. They learn from the cattle and hogs that they raise and slaughter that death is common."

He raised his glass and shot down a Black Jack on the rocks. "He needs killing."

"What?"

"He needs killing."

"Who does?"

"That's a saying, Tony. They use it to refer to somebody they don't like. But more of an insult is when they call someone *common*." I listened intently and made mental notes. Lyle was not only my historian, he was a living, breathing part of what he was explaining. His father had been the county agricultural agent in one of those Acadiana parishes. After a few drinks he found it mandatory to fill me in on how he got into ATF. His education took him into federal law enforcement, first with the old Federal Bureau of Narcotics, FBN, which was a rag-tag, ass-kicking Treasury bureau. It was mostly corrupt but had been the first and only federal agency to identify the mafia as a real criminal organization, even when the FBI under J. Edgar Hoover denied its existence. When the government disbanded the agency, the FBN agents like Lyle were absorbed into the Justice Department's new drug agency that eventually became the Drug Enforcement Administration.

"I hated DEA. They're all backstabbers and social climbers. So I looked around and found ATF as the closest to the old FBN as far as street reputation. And the history of the old Prohibition Unit and Eliot Ness attracted me. I wanted action, so here I am." It appeared that Phil McKinney and Jim King had done a superior job in selecting my contact agent.

CHAPTER 6

We headed west on Interstate 10 for the one-hundred-fifty mile trip to Lafayette where we were to meet the confidential informant the next morning. "Bring me up to speed on our suspect, Lyle. And on the informant."

"His name is Frank Duplessis. He's forty-six years old. We don't know a lot about him other than his record is clean except for a few minor arrests. He trains race horses and runs them at the local tracks. As far as we know he's just another Coon-ass, but a dangerous one who obviously wants somebody dead on his nickel."

"Coon-ass? I thought you Cajuns don't like that term."

"Are you kidding? Years ago it was considered derogatory. A Coon-ass was a backwards, uneducated swamp dweller. But they readily adopted the term instead of being insulted by it and now they use it among themselves to describe the ultimate Cajun, born and raised in Acadiana who adheres to the customs and lifestyle in every way. To many it's simply a proud term they tease each other with."

"How will I handle the language barrier?"

"They'll speak English when they find you're not one of them. If they continue in French, they don't want you to know what's being said."

"What about this informant?"

"The CI's name is James LeBlanc, but everyone knows him as T-Red."

"What the hell kind of name is that?"

Lyle laughed. "T-Red, T-Joe, T-Lou, T-whatever. In Cajun French the T before a name means little, as in Little Red. They use it as a nickname either because of his stature or because he's named after his daddy."

The full moon allowed us a generous look at the vast swamps and bayous that snake their way through the elevated sections of highway approaching Lafayette. Bald cypress trees laden with moss dotted the shallow water pools along the way. We could see the outline of oyster fishermen in their small *pirogues* push-poling their way through the Atchafalaya basin. When we arrived in Lafayette, Lyle picked up a G-car and we drove to a restaurant for breakfast, then at five o'clock we went to meet T-Red LeBlanc in the parking lot of an old abandoned Dairy Queen outside the city. We knew that this was the last time he and I would meet for some time. We discussed the details of where and how to get in touch with each other without blowing my cover. Dawn was still breaking when T-Red arrived in an old, faded red pickup truck with one headlight. The windshield had a crack that ran from under the steering wheel up across to the passenger side. The body had dents that resembled sledgehammer marks. The bed was stacked with bales of alfalfa and timothy. These were not the hay bales of a farmer, but of a race-tracker supplying expensive forage for the elite thoroughbreds racing at nearby Evangeline Downs.

T-Red was short, with a compact build and reddish-brown hair that easily accounted for his nickname. He sported a thick moustache that matched in color. His small but muscular frame and leathered face, coupled with the racehorse feed in his truck, told me right away that he probably was an ex-jockey and one of the exercise riders at the track. He wore the usual backstretch attire of blue jeans, white at the pressure points from wear. His boots showed equal wear but were of expensive brown leather, and he wore a plaid western shirt, topped with a sleeveless insulated jacket which allowed the arms freedom while reining a galloping horse. Although we were in an isolated area on a rural road, his eyes darted back and forth to see if anyone else was around. The old ice cream stand was surrounded by woods, and the nearest anything was a half-mile away on either side. Lyle greeted him in Cajun French and was answered in the same language. He introduced me as Tony Parrino from New Orleans. There was no need for him to know my real name, and he would know me by the undercover identity I had spent several years to establish. Tony Parrino was the name I used because of its consistency with my Italian background, and so I could use my real initials on monogrammed clothing or if I needed to place my initials anywhere.

T-Red crossed his arms and propped a foot on the front bumper of his truck. He started to tell us what he knew about Frank Duplessis and how he became involved in the situation. "Frank is a sour son-of-a-bitch. He's a serious man and I don't take anything he says lightly. He keeps to himself and minds his own business. He has some wealthy thoroughbred owners as clients. He's a crackerjack horseman and knows his shit around the racetrack," he continued. His eyes still surveyed the area every few seconds. He got more nervous as the story went on. "Frank came up to me in the track kitchen and asked me in French if I still hung out at The Gallop. When I said yes, he told me he needed to make a contact there to get a job done. He was kind of evasive at first, but he eventually told me he needed something done that only the boys from New Orleans could handle well." T-Red looked all around once again. "He wants somebody killed."

"The Gallop is a large joint located near Evangeline Downs," Lyle said. "The local police characters hang out there as well as the transient thugs. Dope deals go down and whores are run out of there. Every piece of shit crossing the country from California to Florida by means of I-10 winds up in The Gallop. It's where the assholes of the world meet and greet. Some of the tame race-trackers hang out after the races but, in general, it's a blight. You know, Tony, it's your kind of place."

We both chuckled, but T-Red still had the nervous look on his face. He picked up his story. "Everybody around here who's been around knows that The Gallop is really owned by the New Orleans mafia, although Cliff Dubroc runs the place. Frank Duplessis knows a lot of characters hang out there and he wants me to hook him up with somebody who can do the job for him." T-Red began to shift weight on his heels and weave back and forth, which showed his anxiety was reaching a peak. "Look, I never get involved in this kind of shit. I would normally just blow it off and not say anything to anybody. But knowing Frank and knowing the connections at The Gallop, I know the deal will happen if something isn't done. I don't want that on my head and I don't want to be mixed up in it in any kind of way."

"You are mixed up in it, Red," I told him in a low voice. I stood close to him and looked directly into his eyes. "Frank Duplessis didn't go to a priest for help, he went to you. And he did that because he knew you had the *in*, so let's not bullshit, okay? Maybe you dimed on him because of your concern for your fellow man or maybe just to protect your own ass if the hit goes down. At this point it doesn't matter, because you're in it up to your Cajun ass." T-Red was stunned. He looked at Lyle as if to ask for help of some kind. The first words I spoke to him established my experience and let him know that I was streetwise. I let a few seconds pass for emphasis before I continued. "Here's the deal, Red. I need an intro at The Gallop and around the track. I have a racetrack background but I need you to set me in. We'll pal around together for a while until I'm eased in, then I'll cut you loose and take it on my own from there.

"How long will that take?" he asked.

"That depends on how well we both do our jobs, and a lot of luck."

"What if I bow out and forget this whole deal right now?"

"If you don't go for it, you're on your own and you'd better pray that Duplessis hasn't already made the deal with a killer. In that case, you're under the glass for not reporting a murder plot until it was too late. Are you game?"

"I don't have much choice, do I? I knew when I contacted ATF this wouldn't be easy. I just hope you can cut me out of this as soon as possible. You guys have a lot of balls but you're fucking crazy. Anything can go wrong."

"Nothing goes wrong if you follow instructions." I gave him the phone number at my hotel and told him to call me later that afternoon. Before T-Red left for his work at the track, Lyle rattled off something to him in Cajun French which he acknowledged, then drove off.

"What's that you said about people around here speaking French when they don't want their conversations understood?"

He laughed and said, "Don't worry, I just let him know that if he fucked up he'd have both of us to worry about, I'd cut his ass up and throw it into a nice gumbo." He left in his G-car and I lingered for a minute, breathing in the thick, humid, swamp air. Dust flew from the wheels of my car, along with fragments of oyster and clam shells used as road bedding in that part of the country. I wheeled from the old lot, and drove to the Plantation Inn and checked in. The place was decent and nondescript, was located near the racetrack, and was frequented by horsemen shipping in to run at Evangeline Downs. Lyle had scouted it out as a good place to locate.

I set up house in the hotel on a monthly rate. I caught an hour of sleep, then went to the hotel coffee shop and picked up a copy of the *Daily Racing Form* and thought about the meeting with T-Red. I had met many like him growing up near the Fairgrounds racetrack in New Orleans.

My uncle had trained horses there and brought me on the backstretch when I was six or seven years old. I grew to love the atmosphere and the fierce competition among the horse owners, trainers, jockeys, grooms, hot-walkers, veterinarians, farriers, and others who made their living from the industry. New Orleans has always been a winter racing center, and as a teenager I worked every weekend on the backstretch as a groom or hot-walker, cooling out the horses after the races. After class at Jesuit High School I would go to the backstretch barn, mix the horses' feed, and administer any vitamins or special medication they needed. If we had a horse running in a late race, I prepped him, tacked him up and walked him over to the paddock for saddling. After the race I'd bathe the animal and cool him out, then bandage his legs and feed him. In short, I knew the backstretch routine as well as anyone. My racing career was sabotaged when I became a police cadet right out of high school, working for the department while squeezing out enough credits to earn a degree in criminology from Loyola University.

I also knew that the sport of kings was replete with hustlers, gamblers, cheats, drunks, drug users, and bust-out artists. These characters are generally allowed to thrive on the nation's tracks because they are isolated communities. Only those licensed by state racing commissions can even set foot on the backstretch, and as a rule local police don't patrol the areas or enforce laws there unless called in by track security. This allows many fugitives, illegal aliens, and assorted outcasts to function in this closed society. The situation is tolerated because of the transient nature of the business, with horses and personnel moving from track to track as their seasonal meets open and close. The pay of the grooms and hot-walkers, the backbone of the industry, is quite meager and an ironic contrast to the fortunes spent on many of the horses under their charge.

T-Red fell somewhere in the middle of the spectrum between the ordinary track workers and the wealthy horse owners who throw vast sums of money into the industry. He made his living arriving at the backstretch before dawn, seven days a week, galloping horses in their daily conditioning workouts. Of course, we knew that he supplemented his income by committing petty crime and occasionally ventured into larger scale larceny when the right situation presented itself. I hoped that he hadn't bitten off more than he could chew this time.

I hadn't been back in my room for five minutes when the phone rang. T-Red's voice was a raspy whisper. "I know you told me to call later, but this can't wait. Can you get down with an out-of-town bookie on one of tonight's races?"

"Maybe. What's up?"

"I've been galloping a nag for an old timer who pays me in crawfish because he's got no money. I figured I'd get even if the horse was ever ready to win, and now he is. He's in tonight at long odds. If any serious money is bet at the track, we can't get a good price on him. Can you get a bet down?" He was careful not to identify the horse before he had an answer. A few thoughts came to mind. Was he giving me this tip to set himself in with me? Was he testing to see if I'd make a personal bet or do it in an official capacity? Or, was he simply trying to make a score betting a sleeper who would remain a long shot? My gut instinct told me it was the latter.

"How much action do you want, Red? I have to get it down thirty minutes before post time or it's no bet."

"Bet me a hundred dollars across the board and whatever you can get down for yourself."

"You want me to bet three hundred for you? If this is such a sure thing, how come you didn't go to your mother with the deal? Why me?"

I heard faint laughter over the phone and he answered, "My mama can't get down with an out-of-town bookie. Besides, I don't have the three hundred, and my credit is tapped out with her."

His answer was funny but true, and I told him, "I'll try to get the bet down, but if the horse blows you've got one week to come up with the money before settle-up day with the bookie."

"Deal, Tony. You know I get paid from all the trainers, in cash, on Saturdays and if the old crow blows the race tonight, I'm good for it then. His name is Bob's Dream, third race, number two post position. He loves the rail and unless he gets left in the starting gate he'll go to the lead and he won't look back."

I told T-Red to meet me before the third race in the grandstand, then hung up and shook my head from side to side and smiled. I thumbed the racing form to the entries for the third race. Bob's Dream was an eight-year-old who hadn't finished in the money in his last ten races, except once when he was moved up from fourth to third because of a disqualification. According to his published workouts, I could have run a half-mile in faster time. Even amateur handicappers would eliminate this horse from consideration, and he was sure to pay a big price if T-Red's information was good. I had bet on tips many times before on less information than T-Red had given me. Besides, this was official ATF business. I picked up the phone and called a CI in New Orleans who made his living running a bookie joint. I made the bet and tacked on fifty dollars across the board for myself. If Bob's Dream brought up the rear I'd be out one-hundred and fifty, plus I'd be on the hook for T-Red's three hundred. I thought about how much fun it would be to list T-Red's bet on my expense voucher for the case. If the old horse ran well I'd have a nice windfall and could send my son a belated birthday present.

I finished settling into the room that would be my home for the foreseeable future. After I paid cash for the month's lodging, I had almost two thousand dollars left of the initial cash draw made from ATF for investigative expenses. I peeled out five hundred dollars and put it in my pocket, secreting the rest in the lining of the draw curtains. If the room was searched or tossed, that is one of the least likely and most overlooked places for hidden money. I put away my clothes and killed some time waiting for the night's races by reading the racing form and watching television in my room. I wanted to call home but couldn't call from my room for fear of the call being traced back to my personal residence. I thought about Nick's birthday having recently come and gone without me, and about his laugh. I also pictured Gina's face as it was when I left, her eyes swollen with tears. The cumulative time away from home was taking its toll on our marriage. She was strong and had already put up with a lot, but I knew this assignment put a load on her. The timing was terrible. I could only hope this case wouldn't draw out very long and we could get a quick conclusion.

There was a long night ahead. The races didn't get over until eleven-thirty, and there was no telling where T-Red and I would wind up after that. The Gallop was foremost on my agenda.

CHAPTER 7

I locked my snub-nosed revolver in the glove box and handed the Camaro keys, along with a five-dollar tip, to the valet parking attendant. I didn't like being unarmed but couldn't risk the possibility of being rousted by track security. I walked through the turnstiles at the Evangeline Downs grandstand just as the second race ended. The three-quarter mile dirt oval was well-lit with stadium lights for the night racing that took place. Horses were walked across the infield to come to and from the receiving barns. The track had all the routine accoutrements of the tracks I had been to in the past, but the atmosphere there was distinctively different.

In a corner of the spacious building was a four-piece Cajun band, complete with an accordion player whining the strains of *Jolie Blonde* in French. Listed along with the traditional fare of hot dogs and popcorn at the numerous concession stands were Cajun po-boy sandwiches, gumbo, shrimp, and *boudin* sausage. Small groups of racing fans milled around, their noses buried in their programs or copies of tip sheets and the racing form. Cigarette and cigar smoke hovered over the crowd in a hazy mass. Most of the conversations were in Cajun French. The unusual cadence and pronunciation was only a faint reminder of the fluent Parisian dialect. A few English words were sprinkled in with the unique French brogue. Lawn chairs were placed under the huge grandstand overhang, and scattered all over the paved apron between the building and the racetrack rail. The chairs were owned by the patrons who brought them and set up for close viewing of the races. The fans were relaxed in their seats, grouped around as if on a family picnic. To my surprise, and contrary to most racetrack policies, there were many children there, which added to the family atmosphere. Many of the fans were relatives or personal friends of the jockeys, trainers, and other personnel vital to the operation of the races. Most of them were dressed casually, except for the horse owners and trainers who were distinguished from the crowd by their western shirts and starched blue jeans, usually topped off by a cowboy hat.

When I arrived at the paddock where the horses were saddled for the third race, I saw T-Red talking to several people. He spotted me and quickly walked up and opened his mouth as if to ask a question. Before he could speak I blurted, "The bet is down, Red."

"Hee-ya! What do you think of the old boy?" T-Red's hand motioned to a large bay gelding being led into the number two stall of the saddling area by an elderly man in starched jeans. The horse had good conformation and an intelligent head, but both of his front knees were the size of softballs, swollen by the calcification built up over the years of racing and training. His legs were soaking wet all the way up past his knees, which indicated that the trainer had stood him in an ice tub, an old-time remedy for soreness, in preparation for this race.

"Well, Red, if the old man wasn't trying to win tonight he wouldn't have iced the horse." He looked somewhat surprised by what I said and I could see it register with him that I had worked with racehorses.

"He's trying, and the horse is right. We're gonna cash a bet tonight."

After the trainers saddled their horses in the numbered stalls, one by one the jockeys walked from the jocks' room to the paddock, dressed in their standard patent leather boots, white riding pants, and colorful racing silks unique to each racing stable. They carried leather whips under their arms like field generals past the crowd behind the fence who came to observe the horses being saddled up. The old man gave his jockey a few words of instruction, then legged him up onto the back of Bob's Dream. As the horses paraded onto the track, we waited at the gate where the trainers entered the grandstand. T-Red greeted the old trainer in French, then made an introduction in English. "Tony, this is Alton Comeaux. Alton, this is a friend of mine from New Orleans, Tony Parrino." The old man extended his hand and I shook it, and felt the rough calluses in his palms. Comeaux was in his early seventies, medium height and thin build, and had the leathery face common to many around the track, accented by deep age lines.

"Has he got a chance, Mr. Comeaux?" I asked in a half-doubting, half-hopeful tone.

The old man replied in an accent so thick that I had to strain to understand him. "They all have a chance as long as they've got four legs. But this horse don't have four sound ones."

The cool, crisp night was a welcome contrast to the stuffy, smoky air inside the grandstand. We stood on the cement apron to watch the race as the old man trotted to the row of betting windows. T-Red leaned over close to my ear and said, "Old Comeaux only bets ten dollars, if that much. He's running mainly for the purse money because he's got no cash. It takes all he's got to keep him and the old horse fed." As the jockeys warmed up the horses and made their way to the starting gate, I watched the tote board on the infield of the track and saw that Bob's Dream was fifteen to one in the pari-mutuel betting. T-Red was pleased that his information had not leaked out to the betting public, which would have decreased the horse's odds.

The horses were carefully loaded into the starting gate one at a time. When all were in, there was a pause for a few seconds as the jockeys and their mounts stood like statues and waited for the bell to ring and the gates to spring open. The crowd hushed its usual buzz and waited for the start of the race. Suddenly, the gates shot open and the track announcer shouted *"Il sont partis!"* from the loudspeaker. The strapping bay bolted from the gate in a tremendous burst of speed and quickly galloped a length ahead of the pack, then was settled in on the rail as the horses ran down the straightaway into the first turn. The jockey loosened his grip on the reins, throwing them forward to urge the horse on for more early speed. Bob's Dream increased his lead as the horses thundered into the turn, and when they straightened out for the stretch run, he was four lengths in front of the pack.

"What did I tell you, Tony?" He loves the rail and when he's in front his heart gets bigger and bigger," T-Red cackled.

"Don't count your money yet," I told him as the favorite in the race began a cavalry charge down the stretch. "Lots of sprinters can't hang on in the stretch run." My words seemed like a prediction as the sleek chestnut colt with the number seven saddle blanket gained on Bob's Dream from the outside. As they reached the green-and-white striped pole only an eighth of a mile from the finish line, the old horse was only a length in front. The challenger caught Bob's Dream near the sixteenth pole, and the two horses strode alongside each other so close that from the rail they looked like one horse. The horses strained for each inch of dirt cupped under their hooves. The jockeys rode hard and flailed on the horses with their whips, urging their mounts to give every last ounce of energy. We watched intently as the announcer barked, "And it's Battle Boy up on the outside! Neck and neck to the wire! Bob's Dream! Battle Boy! Bob's Dream! Battle Boy!"

We walked toward the rail to get a good look at the finish. The heads of Bob's Dream and Battle Boy bobbed up and down with each stride as they crossed in front of the mirror at the finish line. It was anybody's guess who won, and either way, only a hair would separate the two horses. We knew it would take the sophisticated photographic equipment and the placing judges to declare the winner. The announcer came on the loudspeaker, "Ladies and gentlemen, there is a photo finish. Please hold all betting tickets until the results are official."

The numbers of both horses flashed on and off the screen constantly on the tote board for several minutes while the judges reviewed videotapes of the race and the finish line photo. The jockeys remained mounted on number two and number seven as the trainers walked them in small circles on the track and waited for the judges to determine which horse would enter the winner's circle. T-Red and I anxiously awaited with the rest of the crowd. Alton Comeaux had a worried look as he continued to walk his veteran of the race wars. The horse bounced with excitement, his nostrils flared from the tremendous exertion. The veins in his neck bulged and his body was covered in sweat. I noticed a slight limp in his gait as he made the circles with Comeaux.

Suddenly, the numbers stopped flashing where the results would be posted, and the tote board was blank for the first two positions. The crowd was silent. Then the board re-lit, with the number two placed on top and number seven in second place. The announcer blared, "After reviewing the photo finish, the stewards have declared number two, Bob's Dream the winner of the third race." The few bettors who had backed the long shot let out a shriek, while simultaneously a low groan came from the many in the crowd who had bet on the favorite, Battle Boy. T-Red replaced his look of relief with an ear-to-ear grin. For the first time, Alton Comeaux's face cracked and he broke into a large smile. He guided his old horse into the winner's circle and patted him on the neck. I felt the same relief and joy as T-Red and Comeaux, and calculated in my head how much Red and I had won. But a stronger feeling came over me. I felt elated by the win for Bob's Dream, for the old campaigner who gave his all, extended his tired old body on sore knees that I knew pinched and hurt with every beat of his hooves. I admired that when he was challenged so strongly near the end, he looked the other horse square in the eye and gritted it out to the finish.

T-Red grabbed my arm to pull me into the winner's circle for the victory picture, but I instinctively pulled back. A hit man surely wouldn't have his picture taken in the town where he'd carry out a contract, or anywhere else for that matter. T-Red and Comeaux hugged as the camera's flash recorded that on this night, in this race, Bob's Dream and Alton Comeaux were winners. There were tears in his eyes as the old man led his horse away, which now limped more noticeably. I wondered if they were tears of joy for capturing the purse money he so desperately needed, or if they were tears of pride and accomplishment for the old horse who gutted out at least one more win. I looked at old Comeaux, who now cried unashamedly, and at T-Red, who was giggling and had taken out a pencil to figure up his winnings. I more easily identified with Alton Comeaux.

Assassin Hunter

CHAPTER 8

The Gallop was situated on Louisiana highway one-ninety north of Lafayette. The building was set in the middle of a huge parking lot and was surrounded by cars and pickup trucks of all types, many of which had parking permits from racetracks all over the country stuck to the windshields and bumpers. In front of the tawny brick building a large, garish neon sign depicted the image of a girl clad in a two-piece outfit sitting inside a champagne glass. T-Red and I still chatted about the big win for Bob's Dream as I made a double pass through the parking lot. Most of the license plates on the vehicles were from Louisiana and Texas, but several were from states like California, Arizona, and New Jersey. Lyle was right about The Gallop being a magnet. I parked and opened the glove box door, which illuminated the snub-nosed. T-Red watched as I stuck the weapon in my waistband in the small of my back, concealing it with an Armani sport coat.

"Hey, maybe you've got a chance tonight," T-Red said.

"A chance for what?"

"A chance to come out of here alive, since you're packing."

"Trust me, Red. I've been in places where they check everybody going in for weapons. If you don't have one, they give you one so you're even with everyone else in the place."

"Then you'll feel right at home."

We both laughed and walked through the front entrance. With the first step inside, I felt the vibrations from a deep blues bass. The smell of stale liquor wafted through the smoke-filled place. The club was large, with a low ceiling, and the darkness gave it an ominous look. It was so dark that it took a couple of minutes for my eyes to adjust, even though we had come in from the nighttime. The walls were made of dark brick, as was the long bar which ran along the left side of the interior. The top of the bar itself had a shiny mahogany finish, and brass foot railings ran along the floor. A platform about six inches in height was at the far end of the bar, big enough to hold the loud band that was beating out a B.B. King tune. In front of the band platform was a medium-sized parquet dance floor, surrounded by a dozen small, round tables. They were encircled by larger cocktail tables. A row of booths hugged against the wall, and the seats and seatbacks were covered in pleated black vinyl. The booths were separated by a four foot brick divider, and they faced another row of booths, which gave that section of the club an air of privacy.

It was almost midnight, and things were jumping in The Gallop. We sat at the bar and T-Red hollered for a beer. "Bloody Mary, extra hit of Tabasco," I told the bartender. He slapped a mug of draft beer on the bar in front of T-Red and stood in front of me to mix the drink. He was dressed the same way as the female bartender at the other end of the bar, in black slacks and vest with a crisp white shirt. T-Red reached into his pocket to pay for the drinks. I grabbed his arm and said, "Fuck it, Red, let Uncle Sam pay tonight."

"I like this, Tony. When I pay my income taxes this year I'll keep in mind where the money was spent."

"Taxes my ass, Red. When's the last time you filed a return?"

"Oh yeah, no shit, Tony. I forgot you were a Treasury Agent. Gonna have my returns pulled?"

"You're safe. When it comes to taxes I can hardly figure out my own return. But, you've given me something to keep in mind in case you ever cross me."

The crowd in the club was quite diverse. Men in expensive suits mingled well with the horsemen in starched jeans. The fedoras, cowboy hats, Kangols, and baseball caps mixed easily. There were about fifteen women in the crowd of seventy-five or so, which grew by the minute. Strong whiffs of cigar smoke strengthened the already stale aroma of cigarettes. The occasional smell of marijuana drifted through the club. The bartenders were constantly busy, working the long bar and setting up drinks for the cocktail waitresses who scurried back and forth to the booths. One of the waitresses, a petite blonde with a page-boy haircut, passed behind us with a tray of drinks. As she did, T-Red wheeled around on his barstool and playfully pinched her on the cheek of her behind, which hung out of shorts so tight they looked painted on.

"Hey, baby, stop back and talk to old Red when you get a minute." She shoved his hand away, and he said in a voice loud enough for her to hear, "Not much tits but what an ass!" Her light-colored eyes scowled, half-ashamed but half-proud of T-Red's crude remark. A closer look at her revealed a light complexion and blue eyes, visible even in the darkness of the room. Her outfit was black shorts and a white shirt tied at the waist, which exposed her midriff. She only paused long enough to brush off T-Red, then continued on to deliver drinks destined for the booths.

"Is our man going to show tonight?" I asked T-Red, referring to Frank Duplessis.

"Probably not, but in this place, who knows? Frank isn't a regular in here, but he steps in once in a while for a drink with his horse owners. He trains for a lot of Texans who like to come in here after the races and make big asses of themselves."

It was just as well that he wouldn't be there that night. I had a chance to break ground and meet a few characters. We ordered another round of drinks, and I reminded myself that I wasn't much of a drinker so my system wasn't tolerant of alcohol. I needed to be alert at all times while maintaining the role and didn't want the booze to creep up on me. T-Red easily slaked down two more beers before I finished the second Bloody Mary. I listened intently as he pointed out several people in the club and gave me thumbnails on the ones he knew. He gave me some background on Cliff Dubroc, the owner, and said that Cliff was rarely around the place at night and handled paperwork and personnel matters during the day.

"Cliff has a low profile," T-Red began. "He runs whores and fences stolen property, and sometimes gets involved in narcotics. He usually stays out of here at night in case the cops turn the joint."

"Then who runs the place when it's hopping?"

"Ritmo. He's probably in the office. He's the head bartender and manages the place. He knows everybody that comes in here."

We were interrupted by a feminine voice from behind. "What the hell do you want, Red?" asked the petite blonde waitress he teased a few minutes ago.

Red turned to her and said, "Some pussy."

"You better keep looking," she replied in a matter-of-fact manner.

T-Red introduced me the same way he had to Alton Comeaux, as Tony, his friend from New Orleans. "This is Cheri, my sweetheart," he said.

She scowled at him and said, "In your dreams."

"Baby, is he always a pain in the ass?" I asked.

She was friendly and laughed, and we chatted for a few minutes until she said, "I gotta get back to work, it's getting crazy in here. Come back, Tony." She gave me a piercing look tempered with a smile, and walked away before I could reply.

"Is she a hooker, Red?"

"Nah. She's a good kid, a civilian just trying to make a living." We hung at the bar for another hour then he said, "Man, I've got to gallop a few nags in just a few hours. Let's blow this joint." I agreed we had done enough for the night, and as we left I took another good look around and made mental notes.

I dropped T-Red off at his pickup truck parked at the track, and went back to my room to make written notes of the night's activities. The detailed notes included the names and physical descriptions of some of the people I met who might become important to the case, and to provide intelligence on them for future cases. I drew a sketch of The Gallop, inside and out, approximated the dimensions of the club, number of employees, tables, chairs, even where the rest rooms were located. I had been on many bar raids and knew this would be helpful if ATF had to raid the club or extricate me in an emergency. Before I fell asleep, the night's activities swirled through my head. I thought about Bob's Dream and wondered if the old horse's knees were still stinging from the race. I thought about T-Red and how to best use him in the next days and weeks. And I thought about Cheri, the pixie-like cocktail waitress, and for some reason felt glad about T-Red's description of her as a civilian. I made no mention of her in the notes I would get to Lyle the next day.

CHAPTER 9

For the next few weeks T-Red and I kept the same routine. We met at the track in the early evening where he introduced me to the local characters, then we hung out at The Gallop for more of the same, hoping to run into Frank Duplessis. Not to my surprise, by the time a week had gone by, T-Red had lost most of the money he'd won on old Comeaux's horse and was borrowing drink money from me.

Each morning I deposited my notes from the previous day in a designated garbage can in the rear service alley of the Plantation Inn. Lyle Melancon retrieved the notes daily from the can, and part of his job was to compile the notes and do whatever backup work was needed. On one of the notes I printed the name RITMO ANGELLE in large letters. He was the manager of The Gallop and I needed Lyle to get a full background check on him. On one of my nightly visits to the club, Ritmo was spending most of his time behind the bar mixing drinks. It was early in the week when the track was closed, and business was slow. The cocktail waitresses were off, and Ritmo worked the bar alone. T-Red and I were nursing a few drinks at the bar, which was particularly quiet because there was no band playing. After an hour or so T-Red made his usual introduction of me as Tony Parrino from New Orleans. Ritmo's attention perked up when he heard this, which in turn made me curious. He had heard T-Red call me Tony many times but didn't seem to pay notice until he heard my last name and that I was from New Orleans. Ritmo asked a pointed question through his bushy mustache. "What are you doing in Lafayette, Tony?"

I stirred the Bloody Mary glass in front of me with my finger and replied, "Following the horses. Unfortunately, I'm following horses that follow other horses."

Ritmo grinned at the joke, which revealed a missing front tooth. He was in his late thirties, of average height, with a powerful, stocky build. His thick black hair and mustache gave the impression that they were painted onto his face and head. A gold earring adorned his left ear, not uncommon among the Cajun men. There was an odd look about him, as if he was a caricature, and it took a while for me to figure out that the look was caused by a bad toupee. I asked Ritmo about Cheri and mentioned that I hadn't seen her in the bar for a few days.

"She only works weekends, keeps a nine-to-five job in town during the week," Ritmo said.

T-Red interrupted. "My name is written on her ass Tony, so chill out."

Ritmo winked at me and said not to worry, as Cheri would be in the following weekend. I was laying the groundwork for having a reason to hang out at The Gallop by showing interest in Cheri, although my interest was genuine. T-Red and I continued with our drinks while

Ritmo was busy at the far end of the bar. T-Red nudged me and pointed his glass at a woman seated in a booth across the floor from us. She wore fishnet stockings and a miniskirt, and sat facing us in a manner that we could see she wore nothing but the stockings under her skirt. She was in her mid-twenties with black hair and dark makeup except for the bright red lipstick. She played with her drink and smiled at us.

A very tall man in his late twenties, clad in jeans and a t-shirt, approached us. He pointed to the girl at the table and asked, "You guys want to party? My girlfriend is hot and it'll only cost you a hundred apiece. One at a time or both together."

We glanced back at her and she winked at us. "Get lost," I told him.

He walked to the end of the bar near his companion, and banged a glass on the bar to get Ritmo's attention. Ritmo had heard him proposition us, and told him to leave. "Take your whore with you. The only hookers in here are ours."

Unexpectedly, the man jumped up and reached across the bar, grabbing Ritmo by the vest with both hands, and shouted something unintelligible. Ritmo tried to break his grasp, but the big guy's height gave him too much leverage. He quickly moved a hand off Ritmo's vest and clutched him around the throat with it. His large, long fingers reached around the entire front of Ritmo's neck. Ritmo tried to pry his fingers loose and at the same time tried to grab a baseball bat that he kept behind the bar. He stretched his hand out of his sleeve as far as he could toward the bat, but it was out of reach. Ritmo's veins began to bulge in his neck and his eyes grew wide.

I ran up behind the guy choking Ritmo and grabbed his elbows together behind his back, which loosened the grip around Ritmo's neck. I swung him around away from the bar and pushed him to the ground face down, then set my knee in his back while keeping his elbows pinned behind him. Ritmo jumped over the bar and slammed his leather boot into the man's neck, letting up only long enough to stomp on it several times, until blood gushed from his ear, which was split from being battered against the floor. He grunted each time his head hit the floor and began shouting "Okay! Okay!" Then, as if we had choreographed timing, Ritmo and I each grabbed an elbow and in a quick-step walked him to the front door, and threw him to the ground outside. Ritmo stared at him and growled, "Don't come back, you motherfucker."

We brushed ourselves off and straightened our clothes as we made our way back to the bar. Ritmo saw me bend over and pick up the snub-nosed revolver, which had fallen out of my waistband during the scuffle. He took his position behind the bar and calmly poured me a fresh Bloody Mary.

"Extra hit of Tabasco, right, Tony? Drinks on me." Then he mumbled to himself, "Goddamn hustlers."

The entire scuffle had happened within a couple of minutes, and took T-Red by total surprise. Obviously shaken by what had happened so quickly, he asked, "Where did you learn how to do that, Tony?"

"In the New Orleans public schools," I answered in a dry humor. We laughed, and Ritmo wasn't aware that I was laughing at his toupee, which had been knocked loose in the fight and was now sitting crooked on his head. What started out as a slow, unproductive night on the case turned out to be quite important, not for the events themselves, but for the friendship I had now forged with Ritmo.

The next morning Lyle woke me up with a telephone call. "Wake up, sleeping beauty."

"Hey, Lyle, what time is it?"

"Ten o'clock."

"Damn it Lyle, it's the middle of the night for me. What do you want?"

"I've got the info on your boy Ritmo. Thought you'd like to know he's a killer. He was convicted of a stabbing death on an offshore oil rig ten years ago. He did a few years in the can, then was paroled and pardoned by the governor. We're trying to find out who his angel was on getting the pardon. He's also keen on stolen property, buying and selling, has a few arrests for it. Is he one of your new pals?"

"This guy might be important, I'll explain why later. Anything else on him?"

"I'll get what I can."

"One other thing, Lyle. I haven't been able to use a cool phone to call home. Call Gina for me and tell her I'm okay. Find out if she got the cash I sent for Nick's birthday."

"Consider it done. Go back to sleep, I know you've got another hard day at the track tonight," He said with a chuckle.

"Hey, Lyle. . ."

"Yeah, Tony?"

"Screw you."

I rolled over and tried to go back to sleep, but despite my efforts to darken the room, sunlight crashed through the curtains and created a beam of light directly into my eyes. I decided to get up and make the most of the daylight hours. I drove to downtown Lafayette for breakfast. The car radio announced that the pack of Democratic candidates for president was beginning to thin out after defeats in recent primaries. I turned the volume up to see if Mo Udall had thrown in the towel, but he was still running. I thought of Ernie Chinn and the protection detail I had left,

..dered if they were still freezing in some remote ..thern city on the campaign trail, while I was in the relative warmth of bayou country.

Around noon I headed for The Gallop. The place was usually quiet during the day and this was no exception. Soft music from the jukebox replaced the loud band. There was only one old geezer sipping a beer at the far end of the bar, and to my surprise Ritmo was working. The place was dark as usual, and the smell of stale, dried alcohol seemed more intense during the daytime. I had experienced this phenomenon many times while checking the bars on Bourbon Street during my days with the New Orleans Police Department. Perhaps the strong smell was due to the fact that heating and air condition units were working at their maximum for the crowds at night but were shut off during the day, or perhaps the liveliness of the crowds themselves lessened the smell. Limited air circulation didn't help. In any case, the remnants of hundreds or thousands of spills, large and small, take their toll after seeping into flooring and furniture. I could tell that The Gallop had its fair share of spills.

I asked Ritmo what he was doing in the bar so early. I saw that his toupee was propped quite squarely on his head as he answered me.

"I was getting ready to ask you the same thing, Tony. I didn't know you drank before sundown."

"Drink? Hell, I'm usually not even up before sundown."

Ritmo appreciated the humor and poured me a drink. I noticed he was drinking coffee behind the bar and yearned for a cup myself. Instead, I was stuck in my role and reluctantly swirled the Bloody Mary with my finger.

A light glowed in the office behind the bar. I wanted to meet Cliff Dubroc and hoped he was in there. After several minutes he came out of the office and stood in the doorway between his office and the bar, only long enough to nod Ritmo inside. He was a short, thin man about fifty years old, well-dressed in expensive slacks and a starched white shirt. He wore thin, wire-rimmed glasses and had wavy, steel gray hair. His physical appearance made him look more like a librarian or chemistry teacher than the pimp and fence that he was. When Ritmo returned to the bar, I pretended to be uninterested in the man in the office.

"Goddamn Cliff is always on my ass," he mumbled as he walked to draw another beer for the old man at the far end.

"Does Cliff take care of you for all the shit you put up with in this place?"

"Fuck no. I do okay, but he rakes it in. I make a few hustles for myself to keep the wolf away from my door. But I'm not bitching. Cliff paid his dues years ago."

I concealed my interest in Ritmo's boss but listened intently to his account of Cliff. By design, Cliff limited his time at The Gallop and my chances to learn more about his activities and to meet him were limited. I didn't know at the time that Cliff Dubroc was equally interested in me.

I looked down at my drink glass and flinched when I tossed down what was left in it. I hated drinking this early in the day and it was a part of the undercover life I had never gotten used to. I knew that a small thing like not drinking the booze I supposedly came in to get could arouse suspicion and put me in question. Constant awareness of making a small slip like this adds stress to the entire equation of an investigation. I got up to leave as Ritmo answered the phone behind the bar and handed it to me.

"It's T-Red, for you."

"How did you track me down, Red?" were my opening words.

"Where else would you be? The track is closed."

"What the hell do you want?"

"I'm helping somebody run a horse in the first race tonight so I won't be in the grandstand until later. We have somewhere to go early tomorrow morning, so in case I don't see you tonight, skip the club and get some sleep."

"So what's the play? You got a hot horse tonight?"

"Hot my French ass. We couldn't cash a bet on this old mare if it was a one horse race. I'm just making a few extra bucks taking her to the paddock for a friend."

"I'm glad to see you're making at least a few dollars on the square."

"Why are you busting my balls, Tony?"

"Okay, okay. If we don't hook up at the track, call me tonight and fill me in."

Ritmo could easily hear everything I said, and although I was anxious to find out what Red had lined up for the next morning, I was careful to give Ritmo as little information as possible. I gave him a goodbye wink and walked out into the bright sunlight. As I approached my car I saw a small Toyota that had seen better days parked next to it. The car had body damage and rust spots in most places, and one headlight was smashed. A diminutive blonde, wearing a smart maroon dress, was seated behind the steering wheel. Her face was buried in her hands and she was crying. I walked up beside the door and asked, "Are you all right?"

She looked up, straight ahead, for a moment. I realized it was Cheri. She didn't answer me and put her head down in her hands.

"Cheri, are you okay?"

She looked up again at recognizing my voice, and remained silent except for the sobbing. Her expression turned to one of embarrassment and shame. I looked into the car and noticed an empty baby seat strapped to the back seat. A few toys were scattered on the floorboard and a carryall bag sat on the back seat. They were reminders of my boy back home.

"Why are you all dolled-up today?" I asked, trying to get her distracted from the crying.

"I'm on my lunch hour from my day job."

"What do you do?"

"I'm a receptionist for an insurance company downtown. My little girl is sick and I just spent my last sixty dollars for her antibiotics that I bought from the pharmacy, and when I got out of the car at the babysitter's house, the bottle fell and broke. I've got no insurance and no money to replace it."

Her words came out so fast that they all ran together. I noticed drops of a thick, pink liquid that had splashed on her black heeled shoes. She sobbed again, "I came to borrow some money from Cliff, but I already owe him a few hundred for repairs to this old wreck."

"Do you get help from your husband? Or should I say ex?"

"That bastard. He left with the horses headed for Chicago when I was six months pregnant, and I haven't seen him since. My daughter is a year old now. The court can't even find him to serve papers."

I got into the passenger side of Cheri's car, leaned over, and dried her tears and running mascara with my handkerchief. I unfolded a hundred-dollar bill and placed it in her palm, then curled her fingers around it.

"Go get your baby her medicine, and get back to work before you get fired." I would have helped her in any event, but I also had the feeling that somehow I was helping a child, someone else's child, which in a strange way compensated for my own failings as a father by being away from my son.

"But, Tony, you don't really know me. I can't take this money."

"You just did. Now beat it."

"I'll pay you back, I promise."

"No you won't. It's a gift. Now get going and take care of your daughter."

The idea of her in debt to a character like Cliff Dubroc didn't sit well with me. If he hadn't been in the club, I'm sure she would have tapped Ritmo, an equally disturbing thought.

A pleasant, almost-smile lit up her face as I slid across the seat and out of her car. She waved, hurriedly threw her car into gear, and made her way out of the parking lot with the old Toyota rumbling from a bad muffler and belching black smoke from the tailpipe. I drove away, amused at how the bureaucrats would categorize that hundred dollars on my expense report, and at the same time I wondered how I would really account for the expenditure.

CHAPTER 10

    The Camaro made its way to the valet parking lane of Evangeline Downs as if it knew the way from the Plantation Inn by itself. I gave the attendant my customary five-dollar tip and decided to watch the races from the clubhouse, since I knew T-Red wouldn't be in the grandstand. I rode the escalator to the second floor, a well-appointed area that was a contrast to the grandstand below that I had frequented on prior race nights. White linen tablecloths covered rows of private tables. Each table had a small television set which displayed the odds from the infield tote board and the closed-circuit viewing of the races. Rich red carpet covered the floor and there were no losing bet tickets strewn around, as was customary in the grandstand. Walnut paneling adorned the walls. A tuxedoed maitre 'd lead me to a private table attended by a waiter who wore a tuxedo shirt and pants with a black bow tie. The clerks manning the betting windows were clad the same way.

Along with the steaks and chops, the menu included Cajun delicacies such as crawfish *etouffee* and fried alligator tail, quite different from the fare of hot dogs and *boudin* sausage vended from the concession stands below. The clubhouse took up the entire second floor of the large building and a wall of glass allowed for a panoramic view of the racetrack. Most of the men were dressed in suits or sport coats and the ladies in dresses. Some wore expensive jewelry. Couples and small parties talked in hushed tones at their respective tables, giving emphasis to the muted sound of the track announcer over the p.a. system. The clubhouse was ornate and had an overall elegant and relaxed atmosphere.

I ordered dinner and quietly watched the first few races from my table, handicapped the horses, and made a few small bets. As the announcer gave one of the usual "Five minutes to post" notices, I walked to the line in front of one of the betting windows. As the line inched forward, I looked up in time to recognize the familiar face of the man leaving the window. It was Luke Trombatore from New Orleans - a member of the Marcello mob, the oldest mafia family in the United States. As a uniformed patrol officer I had assisted the NOPD Vice Squad in a raid on the Rampart Street club named the Glass Slipper, which was run by Trombatore. He operated illegal dice games and a sports book from the club, as well as prostitution in the lower part of the French quarter, and was well known to law enforcement. He was a short, heavy-set man of forty-five with a full head of wavy black hair; cold, dark eyes; and olive skin darkened even more by the stubble of a heavy beard. His upper arms and neck resembled those of a weightlifter and his powerful build had served him well in earning a reputation as an enforcer within the New Orleans mafia.

My initial reaction to seeing him was to glance down at my program so he wouldn't notice me. The surprise at seeing him gave me the feeling one gets when spotting someone without wanting to be noticed. As he walked to his seat at the bar, I realized that although I knew Trombatore, it was an extreme long shot that he would recognize me as one of a dozen uniformed cops in on a raid some years ago. To be certain, I had to take one of the many calculated risks always present in any undercover work. I went to the bar and took a seat next to him. As I studied the Daily Racing Form, Trombatore leaned over and looked on with a cigarette dangling from his lip.

"Who's the class of the race?" he asked in a voice that sounded like gravel being poured out of a tin can.

"Six horse," I replied as I looked him straight in the eye so he could get a good look at me. I wanted to make sure he didn't recognize me.

"Yeah, figures. He's even money."

Without expression, he then sauntered slowly back to the betting window. His lack of reaction told me that he had no clue who I was. I couldn't be sure but all I could do was make the calculated play and move on. I returned to my table and spent the rest of the races there, occasionally trading brief comments about the horses with Trombatore as we passed each other to or from the windows. I observed him the rest of the night to find out who he might be in company with, but he was alone.

After the races I stood among the crowd waiting for their cars to be brought up by the parking valets. I watched Trombatore squeeze his barrel chest between the steering wheel and seat of a new Cadillac Eldorado. As he drove away I memorized the number on his license plate. Before I could get into my car I felt a tap on my shoulder from behind. I turned around to see T-Red clad in his usual jeans and western shirt.

"I'll pick you up at five o'clock at the hotel. Frank will be at the bush track in the morning. This could be your chance to hook up. I know you're a fucking fashion plate, but wear the grubbiest clothes you can muster."

T-Red then put his eyes down and shifted his weight back and forth while stuffing his hands in both pockets, his telltale nervous habit. He let out a short grunt.

"OK my pain in the ass, how much do you need?" I knew he was going to ask me for money.

"I need a grand, but a c-note will do."

"Things are tough all over. I had a rough night at the track myself. Here's fifty. I'll see you in a few hours."

I went back to the hotel intending to skip my nightly visit to The Gallop. Then something came to me. I went to The Gallop and slowly drove through the parking lot, which was filled with cars. Parked among the other cars was the maroon Cadillac Eldorado with the same license plate I had memorized as Trombatore left the track. I was more than curious about him, but realized that a guy like Trombatore would be more likely to hang out at The Gallop than not. I later put the name LUKE TROMBATORE in caps in my daily notes for Lyle to pick up the next day. I requested any current intelligence information ATF or other agencies might have on him or his activities in the area.

Sharply at five in the morning T-Red arrived at the hotel in his pickup truck. I yawned from getting only a few hours sleep and welcomed the cup of coffee with chicory T-Red handed me - the strong, black, murky mixture that was a staple to the Cajuns.

"Frank Duplessis is going to be at the bush track this morning. Yesterday, I told him I had somebody who might do the job he wants. I gave him no name or any other information, didn't want to screw it up."

"Listen closely, Red. Don't say a word to Duplessis unless he approaches us first. You got that?"

"What's the difference? I want to get you hooked up as soon as possible so I can cut myself out of this whole thing."

"Just do what I say."

The pickup rumbled about thirty miles south of Lafayette, past hundreds of acres of rice fields dotted with small tin-roofed cottages. A narrow dirt road took us to a large open field surrounded by a makeshift racetrack. The morning was cold and damp, and there was a misty fog not uncommon in this part of bayou country. There were about two dozen horse trailers scattered about and as many horses in different stages of warming up on the track. Some of the horses were mounted by veteran riders but most were ridden by boys, young Cajuns who were more comfortable on a horse's back than on a baseball field. These were the sons, nephews, cousins, and neighbors of the horse trainers who brought their horses here for training and betting outside of the licensed racetrack. Bush tracks like this are where the nation's top riders like Kent Desormeaux, Eddie Delahoussaye, Shane Sellers, Robby Albarado, and so many more got started in race riding.

"What goes here, Red?"

"These Coon-asses come here to buy and sell, and match race their horses, which they can't do on the licensed tracks."

We walked to the rail and stood among a group of men all speaking Cajun French. In the crowd was old Comeaux, the trainer of Bob's Dream who I had met my first night at the racetrack.

"How's the old campaigner?" I asked.

"You mean old Bob? Well, son, he's enjoying his daily stand in an ice tub up to his shoulders right now. Sore son-of-a-bitch."

"Just think, Comeaux, if you could put his heart into a sound set of legs."

"Hell, we'd win the Kentucky Derby."

We shared a laugh as a large chestnut galloped past us with something I had never seen in my experience around the tracks. A small boy no more than five years old was atop the horse, clinging to the reins, and his legs were tied to the saddle and iron stirrups so he wouldn't fall off. He was the youngest rider there, but not by much. After a few minutes the track was cleared and two teenagers appeared, both saddled onto bay horses. I looked closely and noticed that one of the two horses was a quarter horse. They positioned themselves at the top of the stretch and stood quietly for a few seconds.

"Which one do you like?" T-Red asked me.

"How far are they going?"

"About four hundred yards, a little less than a quarter-mile."

"Fifty says the thoroughbred wins."

T-Red then shouted in French into the small crowd of men standing on the rail. There was some loud discussion and then one of them held some bills high in the air. T-Red grabbed the bills and held them along with the fifty dollars I had given him. He was holding the even-money bet that is illegal on every sanctioned racetrack in America, a match race between a thoroughbred and a quarter horse.

The two riders, who wore baseball caps, turned the caps backwards and inched their knees up into the stirrups. They took up the slack in their reins and coiled their bodies like springs waiting to be unleashed. There was no starting gate and the horses stood flat-footed. An old man standing inside the rail alongside the horses removed his worn straw sun hat and held it up in his hands above his head. When he did, the quarter horse, who was nearest the rail, went into a crouch with his hind quarters. The old man shouted loudly and slammed down the raggedy hat in a quick motion. Both horses took off with the riders screaming and whistling into the horses' ears while thrashing away with their whips. As expected, the quarter horse got out to an early lead and kept a neck in front for the first three hundred yards. As the horses passed the half-way mark where we stood, the pop of leather whips against the horses' hides sounded like firecrackers going off. With about fifty yards to go, the horses drew even and at the finish the thoroughbred had passed his rival by a head. The boy astride the winner whooped and hollered a Doppler effect as he galloped out his horse.

Before T-Red could say a word I slowly took the cash from his hands and folded it into my pocket. At the same time, the Cajuns who were gathered at the rail exchanged cash. As two more horses made their way to the top of the stretch for another heat, T-Red nudged me in the ribs. He cast his eyes toward a man unloading a gray colt from a two-horse trailer. "That's Frank. He's got a two-year-old he wants to test here before working him out at Evangeline Downs."

Frank Duplessis seemed to blend in with the other horsemen. His jeans and shirt were somewhat neater than the others, and he wore expensive Tony Lama boots and carried a Stetson hat. He was rather tall for a Cajun and had a lean, lanky frame. His sad eyes and sun-leathered face, together with a receding hairline, made him appear older than his forty-six years. His arms were long and gangly and swung slowly at his side when he walked. After his horse finished the workout, he joined the others in conversation among the French-speaking men. T-Red and I stood on the edge of the small crowd for some time and watched the match races and workouts. The only conversation Duplessis had with T-Red was the usual bantering and teasing about the horses. T-Red reluctantly heeded my warning not to initiate conversation about me. T-Red helped Duplessis load the gray colt into the trailer and they were gone.

"Let's go, Red. I'll buy you breakfast."

"Goddamnit, Tony!"

"Say nothing. We'll talk about it later."

The sun had burned off most of the morning chill as we headed away from the bush track. We sat at a local diner and I tried to ease Red's frustration about not making the introduction. He had been working hard to set it up and wanted to remove himself from the case. Putting me in direct contact with Duplessis would have gone far in accomplishing that. Although he had become quite relaxed around me, I knew T-Red had other petty action going for himself and I was in his way. He wanted a return to the normalcy of his life as a small-time hustler. I looked square in his eyes to instruct and console him at the same time.

"Here's how it goes. If you or I seem too anxious to meet Frank he could get jumpy. I want him to see me a few times around his own familiar places and people. If he doesn't seem confident in approaching us he might back off. Another problem is what the courts call entrapment. We can't entice him in any way. This has to be Frank's idea, and initiated by Frank, or the whole case could go down the drain."

An enlightened look came over T-Red. The idea was beginning to sink in and he now seemed resigned to the fact that he would be involved for a while longer. However, despite my convincing argument, I realized that Duplessis had failed to seize the opportunity to approach us at the workouts. This opened questions about what direction the whole investigation would now take. Was Duplessis being coy? Was he concerned about his friends seeing him with me? Was he simply too busy taking care of horse business? Or, had our biggest fear been realized – had he already contracted murder with a real criminal? The latter possibility weighed heavy as I recalled my meeting with Luke Trombatore the night before.

Assassin Hunter

CHAPTER 11

"Is dis Tony?"

The voice had the Cajun accent that was more music than language, but it was faint and hoarse by means of a bad connection. I didn't recognize it as anyone who should have my phone number. "Who's calling?" I asked.

"My name is Paul Archambeau, you don't know me. I've got a note here with the name Tony and this phone number written on it. I'm trying to reach anybody who's a friend of Lyle."

"We've got a bad connection. Give me your number, I'll call you right back." The connection wasn't all that bad, but I wanted to buy a minute or two and figure out if the caller was somebody fishing for information about me, or if Lyle was in some sort of trouble. I dialed back and the same voice answered, although it was still hoarse. "Where are you?"

"I'm at a pay phone in the lobby of the Lake Charles Holiday Inn. I was in the lounge here and met Lyle, we had a few drinks together. He left earlier, and I stayed until closing time a few minutes ago. I was on my way to my room here and noticed a dome light on in a car with the door open. I saw a police radio mounted under the dash and a guy passed out on the front seat with a gun in his shoulder holster. It's Lyle. I found his Treasury Department identification in his coat pocket, but thought it best to call a friend before calling his agency. Your name and number is written on a note pad in his billfold."

"Very cool, Paul. Thanks. Tell me how to get there and I can meet you in an hour. Would you stay with him?"

"Sure. He's not going anywhere."

I hurried onto I-10 headed west and wanted to fly low, but couldn't afford a traffic stop or any police harassment. Traffic was heavy for two-thirty in the morning and I did lots of weaving around eighteen wheelers, mostly tankers carrying fuel and chemicals from the plants located on the bays and bayous in the area. I wondered if the call was some kind of setup, or if it was possibly one of Lyle's practical jokes. I shook off these notions and made good time on the interstate, arriving in forty-five minutes.

Lyle's car was parked in front of a first floor room. A man in his late thirties with a receding hairline, compensated by long hair combed over large ears, was standing sentry in front of the car. His slacks, wing tip shoes, and previously starched but now wrinkled white shirt identified him as a businessman or traveling salesman. "Paul?" I asked without identifying myself.

"Yes, Paul Archambeau."

"Is he okay?"

"Well, he's breathing. I didn't want to touch anything after I found out he was a Fed."

The driver's side door was still open, and Lyle was sprawled face up across the front seat. He was fully dressed including a coat, but his clothes were wrinkled. His hair was disheveled and he needed a shave. I leaned into the car, which was filled with the strong smell of alcohol. I checked his pulse, and was relieved when he grunted as I shook him. I found a room key in his hip pocket, and Paul helped me slide the big guy across the seat. He was unable to sit or stand up, so we propped him up between us, pulled his arms around our shoulders, and carried him like an injured football player to his room. We dumped him across the bed, and Paul agreed to stay with him another minute.

I returned to Lyle's G-car and removed his papers, notepads, binoculars, and the backup handgun that he kept in the glove compartment, then locked the car and secured his things in the room. Paul watched patiently as I removed Lyle's coat and belt. I turned to him and said, "Thanks, man. What can I do for you?"

"Nothing, really. I'm just glad he's all right and I didn't have to call ATF about this. Are you an ATF agent too?"

"No," I laughed, "I'm his brother-in-law." Paul nodded and I knew he bought the lie. "You might have saved his job. Can we repay you?" I took a large roll of bills from my pocket. He stared at the money, but politely refused with a negative wave of his hands.

"I hate to see cops get in trouble, even Feds. The press beats up on them, the bad guys beat up on them, the hippies call them pigs and spit in their face. Lyle seemed like a nice guy so he deserved a break."

I couldn't let him leave without finding out if he had learned anything about me, or the investigation, from Lyle. He explained that they had a friendly conversation in French in the lounge, and he didn't even know what Lyle did for a living until he found him passed out in the car.

"I can't check on him later," Paul said, "because I have a six o'clock wakeup for a morning sales call."

"No problem, he'll be zonked out well past that. Thanks again." Satisfied that he was a genuine Good Samaritan, one incidentally with lots of savvy, I showed him the door and accepted his business card. I took Lyle's shoes off, unstrapped his shoulder holster containing the semi-automatic pistol with the ATF badge embossed on the side plate, and placed a blanket over him. I gave him a final jostle and was assured that he was simply plastered when he released a foul, liquor-laden belch. I scribbled a brief note for him to find under his car keys:

Call me when you find out where you are.

Love, Tony

On the drive back to Lafayette, I hop-scotched the Camaro through more fuel tankers and thought about the chink in Lyle's armor. I dismissed thoughts about him drinking when I might need him. After all, he wasn't a backup partner in the pure sense of the term, somebody to respond quickly if I needed help. Working under, there's no such thing – you're out in the cold. You survive with nothing except your own wits and ability. For now, Lyle's *faux pas* would be overlooked. I figured he was entitled to an occasional social error, considering the years of stress he had suffered under sometimes impossible conditions. Despite the transgressions, like an old fire horse he always answered the call. Yet, neither of us needed heat from the Internal Affairs headhunters who surely would have been dispatched to dispense their own brand of justice, had Archambeau not befriended him. We could ill afford to have them running around Acadiana flashing badges to build a trite personnel case. I would surely talk to Lyle about it in the right place and at the right time.

CHAPTER 12

I spent a lot of time at the track and in The Gallop, trying to make contact with Frank Duplessis or Luke Trombatore, without success. It was possible that Trombatore was only in town passing through, and Lyle's check of the police agencies was negative for any current intelligence on him. His last recorded surveillance had been an FBI stakeout of the Glass Slipper in New Orleans two months earlier, which disclosed nothing except that a couple of FBI agents made a few hours overtime watching the place.

Early one evening when the track was closed T-Red met me at The Gallop. One of his army of cousins was having a large crawfish boil, a Cajun custom of steaming the small lobster-like crustaceans and consuming them in large quantities, along with equally large quantities of beer. He had invited me the day before. We met for a drink before heading to the party. We sat at the bar when Ritmo walked over, and after his usual friendly greeting his face turned serious as he addressed me. "I'll bring your drink over to the booth. You can have yours here, Red."

"What's up, Ritmo?" I asked.

"Just follow me."

Ritmo mixed my drink and motioned for the other bartender to handle things behind the bar. I followed him to one of the private booths in the darker section of the club. He set my drink on the table and sat down opposite me on the black vinyl seat. There was anxiety in his voice, which initially made me uneasy. I thought I had gained his confidence, so I wondered if he was going to warn me about some impending danger. I wondered if my cover was blown, and sat quietly and listened. Ritmo got straight to the point.

"I've got a piece of the action on a deal if I can make it fly. You know anything about bonds and securities?"

"Why, Ritmo? You want to invest in the stock market?" I managed a slight smile but Ritmo wasn't laughing.

"Very fucking funny," he growled.

There was a second of silence between us, then I squared up my look at Ritmo and said, "I might know something about that. What's the play?"

"I've got access to some stuff, supposed to be negotiable paper, big numbers. The seller wants fifty cents on the dollar. Are you interested?"

"There's all kinds of paper, Ritmo. It depends on what you've got. I'll have to see the stuff or at least a sample. Then we can talk."

"Tony, this is no chicken-shit deal. How big a bite can you take?"

"Are you fucking deaf, Ritmo? I told you it depends on what you've got. If I can't handle it or I'm not interested, I'll pass."

My answer was calculated to put him on the spot, but I knew it did the same for me. If we went any further, I would get to look at the securities. If he refused to show them to me, the opportunity was lost.

"Okay, I have to make a phone call. Sit tight."

Ritmo left the booth and I noticed that he didn't go to his phone behind the bar to make the call. He walked into Cliff Dubroc's office. T-Red took an occasional glance my way and I could see that he was more than inquisitive about what was happening. He carried his beer over to my booth and sat down.

"What are you bastards cutting me out of?"

"I thought you wanted less involvement Red, not more."

"Not when I smell money. Just keep me in mind if I can get a little piece of it."

"No chance."

My senses heightened as Ritmo came out of the office accompanied by Cliff Dubroc. They approached the booth, and in French Ritmo told T-Red to get lost. I had heard the phrase enough during my time in the area to pick up its meaning. T-Red got up and returned to the bar. Ritmo and Cliff sat down next to each other, opposite me in the booth. My booth was now getting the traffic than others, during the past weeks. I guessed what deals and schemes had been hatched on those vinyl seats. Ritmo spoke the simplest of all introductions in low volume.

"Tony, Cliff."

The professorial-looking pimp extended his hand over the table and gave me a weak, clammy handshake. Cliff's speech betrayed his academic appearance. He spoke in a very thick Cajun brogue and I had trouble understanding some words, even after I had heard the accent daily for weeks.

"What do you know about this shit, Tony?"

"You want me to scope it out for you or are you looking for a buyer?"

"Maybe both."

I didn't know if Cliff had the securities and wanted to sell them, or if he was the buyer and needed expertise to judge their authenticity and value. In order to gain sight of them, I made sure to let him know I was interested either way.

"I need to see the merchandise to know if the paper is real and not counterfeit, and to tell if they're negotiable."

Cliff peered through his wire-rimmed glasses and said, "Come back at eleven o'clock tonight." He rose from his seat and went back to his office. I had set up a possible buy of stolen securities with a man who had said less than a dozen words to me.

"What end are you working, Ritmo?"

"Cliff's. I won't put the bite on you, Tony, but maybe if the deal goes well you'll throw me a bone. I just need to make it happen."

"What kind of paper is it? Where is it from?"

"Fuck if I know. I haven't seen it and wouldn't know what it was if I had." Ritmo was being honest with me. I found it interesting that a convicted killer like him was now brokering a securities transaction, although to him it was just another piece of swag with a bigger price tag.

T-Red and I drove through sparsely populated evergreen country roads to Church Point, a small town in the heart of Acadiana named for its ancestral village in Nova Scotia. It was dark by the time we approached a small house at the end of a dirt road sprinkled with old oyster shells, which the Cajuns use instead of gravel to keep the road from washing out during rains. Spotlights mounted on the rear of the house, which illuminated the large back and side yards. About thirty cars and pickups were parked to one side of the house, and a hundred or so people milled around two long, narrow tables covered with old newspapers. The tables were piled high with several mounds of bright red crawfish releasing steam into the cool night air. Mixed in with the crawfish were small red potatoes, ears of corn, large onions, and whole garlic cloves that had been boiled in with the crawfish for flavor.

Several men attended a large stainless steel pot the size of an oil drum that was heated by a gas grill connected to a large propane gas tank. A tall, rotund man stirred the pot with a large paddle, an oar from a *pirogue*. Occasionally the man whistled, and a teenage boy would submerge a large metal bucket with a perforated bottom into the pot and extract the crawfish. Each time, a large cloud of steam released from the bucket as he hauled it over to the tables and dumped another pile of the miniature lobsters onto the old newspaper. The guests stood around the tables and peeled the coarse shells and sucked the heads from the crawfish to draw out the flavored seasoning. Every bite seemed to require a swig of cold beer from plastic cups, which were constantly replenished by a keg set in a large, galvanized, old-time washtub filled with block ice.

A standard Cajun band consisting of a fiddle, small accordion, bass, and drum played while an octogenarian sang in French. Most of the people held loud conversations in French, laced with an occasional English word or phrase. T-Red introduced me to his cousin, who was the host.

"Meet Gaston, the biggest liar in the world," he said. The large man who had been boiling the crawfish smiled broadly and exposed a missing front tooth.

"You like crawfish, *mon ami*?" Gaston asked.

"I've had them before, thanks. Nice party."

"Hell, we do this all the time. Let me get back to the pot."

"What's the occasion, Red?"

He frowned as if I should know better than to ask. "Cajuns don't need reason to have a *Fais-Do-Do*. We celebrate births, deaths, weddings, good shrimp seasons, winning a horse race, or sometimes just the weather, even if it's bad."

It was now just past winter and the nights were quite pleasant. This one was no exception. Several couples clapped and danced to the whining sound of the band. Children danced with old folks, and teenagers embraced as they did the simple but ancient Cajun line dance. For me the crawfish boil was a welcome diversion from the mental gymnastics of the case. I enjoyed the simplicity and good-natured fun around me and was pleasantly surprised at the genuine, warm welcome I received from everyone. T-Red goaded me into trying my hand at eating crawfish. Although they are plentiful in New Orleans, I had never taken a liking to them.

"Have some mud bugs, Tony."

"Mud bugs?"

"Yeah, that's what we call them. They burrow into the mud in the swamps."

I did my best to peel the hard shells away and eat the meaty tails, which were actually quite tasty, but I refrained on the custom of sucking the heads. I did have a couple of beers which, on top of the earlier drink at The Gallop, gave me a slight buzz. A petite, elderly woman no more than five feet tall approached me. She had short, silver-blue hair in small curls. Her faced carried the lined wrinkles and crow's feet around the eyes that seemed to be a trait among the old people in the area. She spoke to me in French and I looked over at T-Red for a translation, which soon wasn't needed when she extended her arms to me, an invitation to dance. I took her hands and followed her lead, and we bounced to the staccato rhythm of the Zydeco accordion.

She smiled the whole time we danced. I found myself smiling also, and enjoyed the experience as the old lady chattered constantly to me, either not aware or not caring that I didn't understand a word of what she said. I burst out into laughter as the thought came over me that lessons in Cajun dance might be a worthwhile course to teach undercover agents.

Our dance was interrupted by a tap on the shoulder in the manner of an old-fashioned dance cut-in. I turned around to see Cheri standing with her arms extended toward me. The little old lady immediately loosened her grasp on my hands and stepped back. She motioned for me to dance with Cheri, and blushed without stopping her chatter. Cheri stepped into the woman's spot. I continued my clumsy rendition of the dance with her. When the band took a break, we sat on a large ice chest, had a beer together, and I asked about her daughter. Cheri lit a cigarette and took a long drag from it.

"She's fine now, Tony, great thanks to you. I'd like you to meet her."

She took me by the hand like I was a schoolboy and led me to another older woman holding a child on her knee. The little girl was about a year old, with bright blue eyes, fair skin, and long, blonde ringlets. Her face was a smaller, duplicate copy of Cheri's.

"This is Monique."

I got down on one knee to be eye-level with her and smiled. "You're so pretty, Monique, just like your mother." I knew the child wasn't old enough to understand but I said it for Cheri's benefit. Cheri gave me that same half-embarrassed, half-proud look I had seen at our initial meeting. Something about it reminded me of that first night, of The Gallop, and about my real business. I was in this place because it was my job, not because I was there to socialize. My mind jerked back and focused on my meeting with Cliff Dubroc in the next hour. I told Cheri I had to leave.

"You have somebody better to dance with?"

"In fact, I do."

She gave me a puzzled and disbelieving look. I then winked and nodded towards the old lady who had asked me to dance. Cheri let out a long, protracted laugh, then folded her arms and gave me a business-like look. "I thought we might finish the night dancing in private," she said.

I was stunned for a brief moment, unprepared for the proposition. I took Cheri's hand and began dancing as the band played a slow number. She snuggled her small, soft body very close to me as we moved to the music and for a minute I drifted into the moment. T-Red's timing couldn't have been better as he pried my shoulder away from her and stuck his head between us. He spoke to Cheri.

"We got business to take care of. You can play with Tony some other time."

She looked disappointed, but T-Red's interruption gave credence to my dodging her, and, in fact, saved me from having to come up with an excuse without insulting her. We thanked Gaston for the food and hospitality, then drove away from Church Point. My enjoyment of the temporary relief from the case was cut short by T-Red's bitching. He wanted to return with me to The Gallop.

"Let me in on the deal, will you?"

"Forget it, Red."

We got near the club and I switched gears mentally to prepare for the meeting with Cliff and Ritmo. I reached under the car seat and retrieved my handgun, which I had stashed there before the party. I secured it in the familiar place in my waistband, and hoped that I hadn't slept through too many classes on securities during my days at the academy.

The Gallop was rather crowded by the time I arrived. Ritmo was busy behind the bar so I had to wait a few minutes for my drink. As he put it down in front of me he leaned over and said, "Wait a few minutes. Be cool."

"I'm always cool, Ritmo."

Ten minutes later, Cliff Dubroc stood in the doorway of his office with his hands in his pockets. This was the first time I had seen him in the club at night. He stood there quietly for a couple of minutes, surveying the action in the club. I knew that he was also looking for anyone that looked like the heat, as well as whether I had brought anybody with me. He removed his hands from his pockets and went back into the office after nodding at Ritmo. Ritmo then gave a small wave at me to follow him and led me into Cliff's office. Then he immediately left and closed the door behind him. When he did, a confident feeling came over me. Ritmo knew that I usually carried a gun, yet he had not checked or disarmed me before bringing me in. I now knew for sure that I was accepted.

Assassin Hunter

CHAPTER 13

The office was small and cramped. There was a low ceiling of tiles and a single fluorescent light above the desk. An old, large, well-used standup safe stood in one corner behind the desk. An equally old metal file cabinet occupied the other corner. There was a small credenza alongside the wall that matched the old file cabinet. The only semblance of opulence was the large cherry wood desk Cliff Dubroc sat behind. The desk and credenza were covered with sports and racehorse magazines thrown randomly on top of them. The walls were covered almost completely with victory photos of racehorses, some of the pictures yellowed with age and most yellowed from cigarette smoke. Sparse patches of dark paneling peeked through the wallpaper of photos. Cliff Dubroc was in most of them.

"Sit down, Tony," Cliff said as he directed me to the small couch opposite his desk. "Did Ritmo give you a drink?"

"Later. Do you own racehorses, Cliff?"

"No. The fucking racing commission won't give me a license. But I have many friends who own them and on occasion I go watch them run."

Cliff drew a pack of cigarettes from his starched white shirt pocket and lit one with a large flint lighter that was on his desk next to an ash tray the size of a serving platter. There were many old cigarettes, of various sizes depending on when they were extinguished, in the tray. Among the phalanx of horse pictures was a large, gold-framed color photograph of Marilyn Monroe. He pointed to the photo and said, "Look at her. The greatest piece of ass that ever lived."

Surprised at this, I asked him, "You knew her, Cliff?"

"Naw. But a guy has dreams, you know. Some guys still have their Mickey Mantle card from when they were kids. I keep this."

My eyes slowly canvassed the small room, recording mental pictures. I was also looking for any weapons or other contraband which I was sure Cliff had somewhere in the office. He opened the middle drawer of his ornate desk and pulled out a single document and placed it on top the desk. He looked at it for a minute, then stood up and handed it to me over the desk without saying anything. He took his seat behind the desk and waited. I looked closely at the document. It was a ten-thousand dollar note issued by the Commerce Bank and Trust Company of Louisiana. It was a bearer note and was completely negotiable. It had no names assigned and the note belonged to whoever had possession of it. Close inspection indicated that it was printed by the intaglio method, which is also used in U.S. currency because it is extremely difficult to counterfeit. I looked for and found colored fibers that are usually injected into documents at manufacture to insure originality, because they are difficult to reproduce in counterfeits. I was convinced that the note was genuine. The note had a very long alpha-numeric serial number, which was impossible for me to memorize considering the amount of information I had already absorbed in the office. So I used the telephone method, memorizing the last seven digits as if they were someone's phone number. I repeated the number in my head several times before handing the document back to Cliff.

"I've seen it and you've got it. Now what?"

"I've only shown you one document in one denomination. There are more of the same. I know they're real. If you think the same I'll sell them for fifty cents on the dollar, cash money, in any bite you're big enough to take."

"Fifty cents my ass, Cliff. From what I can see the notes are not fake, but they aren't easy to negotiate. Neither one of us can just go to the bank and ask to redeem the notes. They have to be laundered through bogus accounts before they wind up as real money in somebody's pocket. That takes time. And it takes money. Paying half the face value is ridiculous, considering the risk. Not enough profit margin."

"Fifty cents or no deal."

"I'll pass. But I'm around if you change your mind."

He looked at me without saying anything and put the note back in his desk drawer. He knew well that he couldn't get that price for the paper. As anxious as I was to sew him up by purchasing the notes, if I agreed to that price he would either take me for a sucker or suspect that I was an amateur. Either way I'd lose. By taking the action I did, it was now up to him. Even if he didn't sell me the notes, we now knew that he had possession. I wondered how many more like it he might have, where they were, and how he got hold of them. Notes like these are usually safely secured at banks or securities dealerships and don't just float around in circulation. I knew that there was more to this story.

"I think I'll have that drink now."

I got up to leave, and Cliff walked over and opened the door for me. Before I could walk out, he said in his thick accent, "We might talk again."

CHAPTER 14

I didn't leave any notes for Lyle to retrieve from the garbage can the next morning. I stayed up a few more hours to call him before his pre-dawn visit to the refuse alley of the Plantation. At four o'clock I rang his phone.

"Is this the Sanitation Department?"

"What are you doing waking me up? Four-thirty comes early enough."

"Forget today's garbage run. We need to meet, give me a cool place."

An hour later we were sitting across the table from each other in the Lafayette Hilton coffee shop. Lyle wrapped his paw around a hot coffee mug and leaned toward me to listen. I dispensed with the usual jibes and told him about my meetings with Ritmo and Cliff and about the securities. He jotted notes as I laid down the proposition. I pushed across the table the only written note I had for him, which contained the memorized last seven digits of the bank note Cliff Dubroc had shown me.

"These notes are the real deal. They're bearer instruments, payable on demand to the holder, regardless of who they were originally issued to."

"Any idea how Dubroc got these notes?"

"No, but we should be able to find out how they got into circulation." We surmised that they were stolen in a burglary of a bank or securities dealer. Perhaps they tapped them from a private safe deposit box or bank vault. It was even possible that the owner didn't know they were missing. We knew that with the origin of the securities, we would be able to piece together how they got into Cliff's possession and the identity of others who might be involved with them. We were in agreement that Cliff didn't have the finesse or the balls to be involved in the actual acquisition.

Lyle handed me a teletype dispatch sent to ATF from Interpol. When headquarters traced down the notes, the international police agency requested any information we had on the bank securities, which are the type usually negotiated more easily outside of the United States if they're stolen.

"What about this? They aren't giving Interpol any information until we have them in hand, are they?"

"Not yet. But it generates more pressure on the brass – speaking of which, what's the progress on our main target? I'm getting lots of questions from the ivory tower."

"I've met Frank Duplessis but he hasn't approached me about the contract hit. I can only wait until he makes his move or else chance blowing the deal. Hey, what questions?"

"Take it easy, Tony. I'm fading all the heat. They just want to make sure Uncle Sam is getting his dime's worth. You're making my job harder with some of the unorthodox crap you've been listing as expenses."

"Then I guess they'll flip over the dollar I spent last night for a condom."

Lyle stared at me for a long moment, then said with a straight face, "You're giving new meaning to the term 'deep undercover'."

He was glad we met for several reasons, one of which was to move other business off his list of things to tell me. He gave me a piece of paper with a phone number for Ernie Chinn from the Secret Service and said he tried to reach me a couple of times. He also told me he had spoken to Gina, that she and Nick were fine.

"She sounds great, Tony, but I think she's putting up a little bit of a front. She's anxious to talk to you whenever you can call."

"Call her back for me and promise I'll call this weekend."

"I gave her that message two weeks ago. You didn't call her, you bastard?"

"I couldn't," I muttered." Do your best to explain, will you?"

I knew this was a lame way to put the matter off, but I was trying hard to maintain the role without family distractions. I promised myself that, no matter what, I would make a long phone call home.

"Lawyer the case for me, Lyle. I'm sure you've still got a few sweet words left in you that can soothe the savage wife. Now what else have you got?"

"We put a couple of agents on Luke Trombatore. He's been back to New Orleans twice since you ran into him at the track. He was seen with Carlos Marcello one afternoon, otherwise no activity that can help us out. We haven't been around-the-clock on him but it looks like he's got more than a passing interest in Lafayette. The ivory tower wants you to move him up on your priority list."

"Trombatore meeting with the mafia boss wasn't of interest? I've got the same feeling the tower has about Trombatore from my vantage point. He's not just out here playing the ponies."

Lyle caught me up on the routine ATF news, and we chatted for a while about the upcoming major league baseball season. Before leaving he asked, "How's the snitch?"

I knew from prior conversations that Lyle didn't like informants, the necessary evil of our work. His tone reflected the feeling of the love-hate relationship all agents have with informants. "T-Red? He's okay, as CI's go. Anxious to get out. He's a money sieve. This guy destroys money. What a pain in the ass."

"That's why I never work undercover unless I have no choice. I hate snitches. I have my own. I tolerate them, but you undercover guys put too much faith in them. I've watched too many agents go down, here with ATF and back in the old Federal Bureau of Narcotics, because of some two-faced, sleaze-ball informant. If they don't get you killed, they get you fired."

In a matter of hours my words, as well as Lyle's, would prove to be un-exaggerated. Lyle stood up to leave, then leaned his hulking frame over and rested his hands on the table in front of me. As if a professor speaking to his student he said, "I'm glad you're staying focused, Tony. Keep your head in the game. But stay in touch with those at home. I've been around long enough to see the carnage of families broken by the job."

I didn't answer. His words echoed. He left, asserting that he would call me as soon as information developed on the bank securities. I remained for a few minutes, thinking about the phone calls I needed to make in order to catch up with my personal life. I hadn't phoned in weeks. When I arrived at the Plantation, T-Red was waiting in front of my room.

"What are you doing here?"

"I need a favor."

"Sorry, Red. No money."

"No, not that. My truck broke down and I need a ride downtown."

"Forget it, Red. I haven't been to sleep, and I'm going in that room to crash. Besides, I'm not a taxi driver."

"C'mon Tony. Ten minutes to downtown, ten minutes back. Do this, will you?"

I thought about it for a moment, and realized this would be a favor I could do for him that wouldn't cost money. My meeting with Lyle had reminded me about the bean counters in the agency and their concern over expenses. I reluctantly agreed. I noticed that he was dressed in a golf shirt and dress slacks instead of the standard jeans and western shirt. His worn leather boots were replaced by oxfords, and his hair was neatly slicked back.

"You look like you're on your way to make your first communion," I told him. "What's up?"

"I need to make a past due payment on my account at Abdalla's. If I don't do it today they'll shut off my credit."

I followed T-Red's directions to the central business district of Lafayette. I pulled up to the curb in front of the main entrance to the upscale department store. T-Red leaped out of the car and said, "I'll only be a few minutes, keep the engine running." He bounced into the store through the large glass revolving door.

I sat behind the steering wheel and admired the expensive suits and silk ties on the male mannequins in Abdalla's large display window. I watched the pedestrian traffic and tried not to fall asleep, but my efforts were futile and I began to fade. I was in the state of half-awake, half-dozed when, without warning, I was jolted awake when T-Red jerked open the car door. He jumped into the front seat like an athlete, while simultaneously throwing a large swatch of clothing into the back seat. He slammed the door behind him and yelled, "Let's get out of here, quick!"

I wasn't sure what was happening but the suddenness of it all kicked-in my sense of inherent danger, and adrenaline took over. The engine of the Camaro roared as I floored the accelerator and sped through the red light at the end of the block. My mind raced with thoughts of shots being fired at us or worse. I wasn't sure why, but I knew we had to get away as soon as possible. The situation became clearer as I looked in the side view mirror and saw a well-dressed salesman and a uniformed security guard run out of the store entrance in our direction. Their figures diminished quickly in the mirror as we headed away from downtown at a high rate of speed. My heart pounded and breathing got heavier as I weaved in and out of traffic. T-Red screamed when I swerved to avoid hitting a young woman who stepped off the curb to walk her child across a busy intersection. After a few minutes we were in normal highway traffic and I began to compose myself, knowing that we had escaped. But escaped from what? I pulled the car into an alleyway behind a strip shopping center. When I was sure we were out of public sight, I slammed the car to a halt. T-Red and I hadn't said a word to each other during the entire trip away from downtown. I looked into the back seat, and there was a dozen or so men's cashmere sweaters, in an array of pastel colors, each with an Abdalla's label sewn into the neck. There was a two-hundred dollar price tag attached to the sleeves.

Within a split second, it was all clear to me. T-Red had boosted the sweaters from the swankiest store in town and had used me as his getaway. I was enraged, and felt the veins swell in my neck. My face flushed, and the muscles tightened all over my body. I reached over and grabbed T-Red's shirt with my left hand, and drew back my right fist and drove it into his jaw. Blood jetted onto the passenger window as his head swiveled from the blow.

"You sonofabitch."

T-Red protested little except for putting his arms up and curling his knees in self-defense. When he finally uncoiled and dropped his arms enough to peek through, I slapped him in the face with a back-handed open fist. My index finger scraped against his teeth and it began to bleed at the same time as his lip oozed blood. My anger was directed at myself as much as at him. I was mad for having lost control of my informant, for being used and taken in a direction that endangered the investigation.

I slowly pulled myself together and wrapped a handkerchief around my finger. I got out of the car and walked around back to get some fresh air and cool off. After a minute, T-Red joined me outside the car, holding a pale yellow cashmere sweater against his face to stop the flow of blood. Much of it was stained red from blotting the wounds to his face.

"Listen, Tony. I didn't set you up, this wasn't planned at all. I went inside and made my payment so they wouldn't shut off my credit. When I was walking out through the men's department, there they were, stacks of cashmere sweaters piled high on the display table only a few steps from the door. The score was too easy to pass up. I scooped up an armful, and a few seconds later we were gone."

"You could have gotten us pinched, or even shot, you little prick."

At first I gave no credibility to his explanation. Then I began to wonder. We had worked so closely for so long that T-Red may have crossed the line that some agents cross, not being able to separate the good guy from the role he's playing. Maybe I had done too good a job as far as T-Red was concerned. After all, Ritmo and Cliff Dubroc had certainly bought the act after approaching me to buy the stolen securities. I needed to know more in order to assess what happened.

"What were you going to do with this swag?"

"With the labels removed so they can't be traced, I can get fifty bucks apiece for them around the track. We'll cut up the score straight down the middle. Why are you pissed? Do you think old Red would cut you out?"

I couldn't believe it. He still didn't give a damn about jeopardizing the case or my career, much less our lives. Considering that we could have been shot during the wild getaway, we were fleeing felons endangering the lives of civilians. We got back in the car and I drove to his truck in the parking lot at Evangeline Downs.

"What are you doing, Tony? I wasn't bullshitting about the truck breaking down."

"Tough shit. Get out."

He reached across into the back seat to retrieve the sweaters. I stuck out a hand, grabbed his arm tightly and said, "Don't even think about it."

Before he could say anything, I snatched the blood-drenched sweater from his hand, which was now only yellow at the wrists. I slammed the door and drove away quickly. On my way to the hotel I ditched the bloody garment in a garbage dumpster placed behind a super market. I brought the rest of them into my room and threw them onto the bed. I took a quick shower, and slouched in an armchair while thinking about what to do with T-Red and the sweaters. The lack of sleep, combined with mental and physical exhaustion, put me in slumber land.

I slept for what seemed like a few minutes when the

phone rang. A glance at the clock told me I'd been asleep for two hours. Still groggy, I wobbled slowly over to the phone, sat on the edge of the bed, and murmured "Yeah," into the receiver.

"Jackpot!"

The pitch and volume of Lyle's voice finished waking me up.

"Those bank notes are hotter than a two dollar whore's ass. A half-million dollars worth were taken in a bank robbery in New Orleans eight months ago."

"Bank robbery?"

"You got it. But that ain't all. An off-duty cop working overtime as a security guard was killed in the heist, shot between the eyes during a hellacious gunfight in a bank lobby. He left two kids, grieving widow, slain officer's funeral, the whole bit. His name was Bobby Cazale', well thought of in police circles.

"I didn't know Cazale', but I heard of the case. We need to get those bank notes."

"These guys were brazen - broad daylight, walked in with guns drawn, nailed the cop before he knew what happened, caught them with the vault open and got two hundred thousand in cash and the bank notes. One of the shooters was apprehended a week later. He's in custody awaiting trial but he won't give up the accomplices. None of the money or notes has been recovered. The bank note you saw is the first of anything that has surfaced."

"Holy shit," I replied in a low monotone. "Poker just went up."

"Sit tight. The ivory tower is trying to figure out which end is up. For now you're supposed to change nothing. But you'd better get a handle on the Duplessis contract before this securities thing takes on a life of its own."

"Check. Get back to me soon. And Lyle, get me a new

license plate."

"For what?"

"This one may be hot. I'll explain later."

"Later, later, later. I can fill a book with things you'll explain later. I hope you know how much I'm covering for you."

"It all goes toward a twenty year pension. Besides, we're even. Remember the Holiday Inn?"

"I'm trying to forget," he laughed. "I'll get a cool plate that matches your car and leave it in the drop spot tonight."

Lyle went on to explain how the FBI and NOPD had a task force working on the bank robbery/homicide but were unable to come up with much other than the shooter, James Bratton, who was a common street thug with enough bravado to pull a bank robbery and execute a cop. Otherwise he was a mope, but they suspected more intricate involvement by higher-level criminals. The silence of the man in custody wasn't unusual, but the theory that he was low on the food chain in this job was bolstered by his obvious fear of talking. After eight months of interrogation supervised by his attorney, he was a dead end. ATF kept its hand in the investigation by tracing the gun used in the robbery. The trail ended when it was traced back to a local pediatrician who had it stolen in a Garden District house burglary a few days before the robbery.

Lyle seemed in a hurry and said, "Later, brother. I've got to get busy on your license plate and get to New Orleans for a meeting with the SAC on this thing. The stakes are higher now, watch your back."

His statement about the special agent in charge reassured me. Jim King would be involved in calling the shots. His extensive undercover background before rising through the ranks would bode well in protecting me and the investigation from the bureaucratic squabbling that would surely ensue. ATF had to decide how much, if anything, we would let the Federal Bureau of Investigation, Interpol, and the New Orleans Police Department in on. Things would get sticky at the upper level, and Jim King would be only one voice in the internal strategy meetings with ATF command in Washington.

My plate was filling up quickly. I had to deal with the T-Red situation, keep negotiations open with Ritmo and Cliff about the securities without pushing too hard, and get to the bottom of the Duplessis contract murder. I freshened up, and picked up the former contents of my coat pocket off the dresser, and transferred them to my jacket for the evening. The note from Lyle with Ernie Chinn's phone number was lying on top the small pile of pocket change. I decided to try calling him, although chances were always remote that our schedules coincided enough to make contact. I was pleasantly surprised when his familiar voice answered, but wasn't quite ready for the greeting.

"Chang's delicatessen."

I hesitated momentarily, then answered, "I want two corned-beefs on rye. Hold the mustard."

Ernie responded in his boyish chuckle, "Hello, Muss. How's things in wherever the hell you are?"

"Getting a little hairy, but under control. What's with this Chang's Delicatessen?"

"You think ATF is the only outfit that does sneaky shit? It's our undercover phone line, the cool number."

"I got your messages Ernie, but..."

"Yeah, yeah, I know how it is. Glad you got to make this call. Besides making sure you're still around to buy me that lunch you owe, I wanted to let you know that Big Mo is dropping out of the presidential race. He'll officially announce tomorrow. I'm already off his detail, playing office boy. Tomorrow I'll be sipping evening martinis with

Rocky."

"Great. Too bad you'll still be on the campaign trail, but Air Force Two is quite a step up from the piece of crap we flew with Mo. Thanks for the heads-up, Ernie. I don't know when we'll talk again, but stay in touch with Lyle. He's ace."

"I can tell, Muss. Glad he's your contact. Take care."

Senator Morris Udall, my former protectee, was throwing in the towel in the Democratic presidential campaign. Ernie Chinn was being assigned to the protection detail of vice-president Nelson Rockefeller, who was campaigning hard with his running mate, president Gerald Ford. The call to Ernie reminded me that just weeks before, I wore a three-piece suit every day, stood among powerful government officials and elite politicians on the national scene while on protection detail. Now I was an accomplice to grand larceny and an accepted member of a sleazy underworld. All for the same paycheck. I finished dressing and headed to the track. As I joined the small crowd waiting for the escalator up to the clubhouse, I felt a large, powerful hand clutch my shoulder from behind. It felt like vice grip pliers, and as I turned around the pressure from the stubby fingers released as quickly as it had come. It was the hand of Luke Trombatore. He was clutching the *Daily Racing Form* in his other hand, and was accompanied by a nattily attired, steely-eyed younger man who was picking up the valet parking ticket for Trombatore's Eldorado. The shoulder grab was a greeting. As he let go of my shoulder, his raspy voice addressed me, *"Buona sera, paesano."*

CHAPTER 15

"*Buona sera. Come' stai* ?" I replied to Trombatore as we rode the escalator to the second floor clubhouse.

"Not bad, except I need a winner. Any information?"

"I get a hot horse once in a while, but I'm mostly picking my nose."

Trombatore gave an understanding grunt and walked to a table where he was seated with his younger companion. I took a seat at what was by now my regular table, which faced theirs only twenty feet away. As the waiter set up my table I studied the man with Trombatore. He had an intense look and seemed to be more interested in Trombatore's needs than in betting the horses. He was dressed in a suit that looked like the standard uniform of a Las Vegas pit boss - expensive, well-tailored, charcoal gray suit, with a matching monotone shirt and tie, and Italian leather shoes. He was somewhat taller than Trombatore, about thirty-five years old, medium build, with neatly styled dark hair and a medium-dark complexion. He sported a gold bracelet on one wrist and on the opposite hand, a diamond pinky ring.

A few minutes after I was seated, the waiter delivered a bloody Mary to my table and nodded in the direction of Trombatore, indicating that it was with his compliments. I looked over at him and the charcoal suit, and they were both holding drinks. I picked up the cocktail, held it up in a gesture of thanks and the three of us toasted as Trombatore bellowed "*Saluta.*" During the evening we passed each other's tables to and from the betting windows and traded small talk about the horses, except for the charcoal suit who didn't say a word to me, as if he didn't have permission or was being dismissive. He ran bets to the windows and was coming into focus as Trombatore's driver-bodyguard.

After the first race, the waiter brought a telephone to my table. I took the call and T-Red's voice was on the other end.

"You still love me?"

"I shouldn't even talk to you, asshole, but what do you want?"

"I'm gonna make things up to you right quick. There's a five-to-one shot in the next race that can't blow. He's been running blistering times in the morning workouts and the clocker has kept these times out of the official publications. Unload on the six horse."

"I'm not betting a dime for you, Red."

"Don't want you to. This is a ta-ta," he chirped as the phone clicked dead.

I glanced at the program and *Daily Racing Form* to discover that the horse indeed had no fast published workouts and appeared as if he was only running to round out the field. After handicapping the other horses I decided that if T-Red's information was correct this would be an easy score. More importantly, it gave me a reason to approach Trombatore's table. I walked over deliberately and sat down across the table from him. He peered over his racing form with the ever-present cigarette dangling from his lip.

"Six horse. It's a clocker's special. Tie him up with exactas so the win odds won't shorten up."

He knew better than to ask me for more information about the tip, but I was sure that he noticed me take the phone call at my table. I got up as quickly as I sat down, but not before getting a good look at the pinky ring on the charcoal suit's finger. The initials "P T" were laid out in small diamonds on a gold band. This was easy enough to remember. I went to the betting window with the charcoal suit following behind, and bet a hundred dollars across the board on number six, laying three one hundred-dollar bills in the window. I couldn't see how much he bet without being noticed, so I returned to my table.

As the horses lined up in the post parade, the black colt bearing the number six saddle cloth pranced his way to the starting gate along with the rest of the field. The infield tote board showed his odds at four to one and holding, so the information had not leaked enough to pull the odds down. The horses were soon in the starting gate as the customary *"Il sont partis"* came from the track announcer. Since the race was at a distance of a flat mile, the early pace of the race was slower than the sprints, and our horse was galloping easily in the middle of the ten starters around the first turn. He remained in that position down the backstretch, and as the horses went into the final turn, he began to drag the jockey to the lead, despite the rider's efforts to pace him. The jock then went with the horse's power, guided him to the outside around the field, and then from there the black horse drew away on auto-pilot to an easy five length victory. The jockey never used his whip. It was a textbook score, and what made it sweeter was that the even-money favorite finished second, which made winners out of the exacta bets.

"Ladies and gentlemen, the results are official."

The track announcer's words gave us the green light to cash the winning tickets. I purposely wound up in line at the cashier's window behind P.T. and looked around his shoulder to see the clerk counting out a large stack of one-hundred dollar bills. The total came to an odd amount and he left a twenty on the counter for the clerk. He scooped up the rest and delivered them to Trombatore, who peeled off the first two large bills and shoved them across the table to P.T. I returned to my table to find a fresh drink waiting, compliments of Trombatore. As before, I raised my glass simultaneously with Trombatore and his bodyguard, who were both smiling for the first time that night.

This time the toast came from P.T., who murmured, "*Cent'anni*" in my direction.

After the races I went directly to my room. I figured that Trombatore would show up at The Gallop, and I didn't want to go there and rush my acquaintance with him. The phone rang as I entered the room. I picked up and said, "Well, if it isn't T-Red."

"Yeah, who loves ya, baby?"

"You said this was a ta-ta, Red. What do you want?"

"Well kinda, Tony. I don't want anything from whatever you scored tonight, although you must admit the information was primo. But, I was wondering what you're gonna do with all those cashmere sweaters?"

"You're un-fucking-believable!"

While I listened to T-Red hustling me for the swag from Abdalla's, I jotted down a description of Trombatore's clothes-horse companion and the initials "P.T." for the notes Lyle would retrieve in the morning. I then diverted my attention back to the phone call and told T-Red. "Be here in fifteen minutes." A few nights later at the track, I was surprised to see the parking valet pick up my car wearing a peach-colored, pullover cashmere sweater. I immediately recognized it from the stack I had returned to T-Red. As I exchanged my keys and usual tip for the parking ticket I told the valet, "Nice threads." He plopped behind the wheel, and I reached over and turned up the back of the sweater behind the neck to see if there was a store label sewn inside. T-Red had neatly removed the tag. The boy gave me a strange look for a second, then drove off to park the car in the reserved lot.

From my seat in the clubhouse that night, I saw a dozen or so trainers, grooms, and tote clerks wearing the same style sweaters, in a lovely array of pastel colors. At first, as I noticed each one my temper rose, but after a while it became amusing. By the end of the night I saw the porter sweeping up discarded bet tickets from the floor wearing one in mint green. T-Red had wasted no time unloading the swag, and I hoped the men's department salesman from Abdalla's did not frequent the track. I was also pleased that T-Red now had a few bucks and wouldn't be hitting me up for money, at least for a while.

Luke Trombatore and P.T. hadn't shown up in the clubhouse for a few nights, including this one. For the first time, I saw Ritmo Angelle at the track, standing by the clubhouse bar studying a racing form. I caught his attention and waved him over to my table.

"Let me buy you one for a change, Ritmo. Are you off tonight?"

"Yeah, just killing a few hours before the graveyard shift. What's happening on the deal with Cliff, Tony? I'd sure like to see this thing happen."

I was glad to hear the question because it meant that Cliff Dubroc still had the securities. I lowered my voice and told Ritmo, "Sure, I know you've got a piece of it for brokering the deal, but business is business. I made an offer, he turned it down. I'm sure Cliff knows that the value of those notes depends on how hot they are."

Ritmo was working on Cliff as hard as on me to put the deal together. I wanted him to bring this information back to Cliff. I didn't know if Ritmo knew the history of the notes, but surely Cliff did. If I paid his price I'd be a double sucker in his book, first for paying more than they were worth on the black market, and secondly for taking the hottest paper in America off his hands.

"Come by the club tonight," Ritmo said as he left for his job at The Gallop.

"Think I'll pass tonight, not feeling well."

I wanted him to bring the information back to Cliff without my being there. I also didn't want to run into Trombatore and his bodyguard until I knew more about P.T. If they were still in town, they would show up at the track soon enough.

The waiter brought a phone to my table and set it down. Expecting T-Red to be on the other end, I picked up and said, "Abdalla's men's department."

"What the hell is that all about?" Lyle Melancon shot back. "Never mind, I don't want to know. Call me from a pay phone."

I left before the last race finished and headed for the pay phone in the lobby of the Plantation Inn. Lyle was his usual, efficient self and he got to the point.

"P.T. is a guy named Phil Tanzini. Connected, a few busts. His rap sheet shows a fall for narcotics, which makes him a convicted felon. The brass would love to catch him holding a piece. ATF is hot to trot on felons with firearms, especially mob guys."

"We've got lots of time on that, Lyle. It shouldn't be tough to catch him holding. Any moves right now will chill whatever is happening with Trombatore. Tell the brass to be patient."

Lyle went on, "Tanzini has turned up frequently in Trombatore's company in surveillance reports. He's a rising star in the mob, known as the *Ice Pick*, a little nickname he got from carrying one concealed."

"This guy carries a fucking ice pick?"

The thought of this somehow made Tanzini more dangerous than if he carried a gun, although I'm sure he was no stranger to that. I had seen two separate murders with ice picks when I was a cop. In both cases not even a drop of blood came from the wound, yet vital organs or lungs were punctured, causing death from internal bleeding.

I deadpanned, "Check the ATF regulations and see if we can bust him for being a convicted felon in possession of an ice pick."

Lyle gave out one of his deep chuckles and finished by saying, "He's being groomed, no telling what kind of finer points he's learning from Trombatore. That's it for now, Tony. By the way, when are you going to call home? You're at a pay phone right now."

He was right. I was standing in a phone booth. Although it was midnight in Miami I hoped Gina would be awake. I threw a pocketful of change into the phone and called. She answered in a voice that was energetic and upbeat. In fact, she was laughing as she answered.

"Hey, babe, what's so funny?"

"Watching the Tonight Show," she said matter-of-factly as if we had just spoken to each other the day before.

"Sorry I haven't called, but . . ."

"Hold on." I heard the television click off and Gina's voice was now louder and softer over the phone.

"I miss you. Nick asks for you every day."

"Tell him when I get back we're going to Disneyworld."

"Hell, no."

"No?"

"No. When you get back we're just going to catch up and do normal things like normal families around here – work in the yard, go to the park, take Nick to a baseball game. Got it, hot shot?"

"Yeah, sounds great."

"Did Lyle tell you about the checks?"

"What checks?"

"ATF didn't send your paychecks here for a month. I had to put everything on credit cards."

"*What?*"

"It was embarrassing, Tony. I had to get cash advances on the credit cards just to have money in my purse."

I was so angry at hearing this I clenched a fist and pushed it against the glass of the phone booth. I was out here exposing my ass for the government, and my wife and kid had to scrounge around for money because the agency couldn't handle its business right.

"Wait till I get those bastards on the phone!"

"Calm down, Tony. It's all straightened out, thanks to Lyle. He now picks up the checks and sends them to me. You've got a great pinch hitter in that guy. He's done everything I've asked except fix the kitchen faucet, and I think he'd do that if he wasn't a thousand miles away."

The conversation then turned to household bills, the nosy neighbor who was constantly curious about my long absences from home, and extended family matters. The sound of Gina's voice had a soothing effect on me and reminded me of my real life, and how much I missed it. She asked if I was eating right and on schedule, and I lied.

"Yes, of course." I almost made a comment about the abundance of wonderful Cajun food, then remembered not to give her too much information on where I was. We exchanged kisses on the phone and I made the usual promise to call soon. She had not asked me when the case would be over or what it was about. She spared me the anguish of making up answers or trying to give answers I didn't have.

"Next time call when Nick is awake."

"My time is up on the phone and I'm out of change. *Ti amo.*" As the phone went dead it reminded me of the detachment from my family and real life, and threw me back into reality, to the phone booth at the Plantation. I walked down the narrow hall to my room and felt the guilt of not being home and of the hardships placed on Gina and Nick. I wondered if the case was worth it, if the job was worth it, if anything happening here really mattered at all.

Assassin Hunter

CHAPTER 16

I was awakened by loud rapping on my door. The room was still dark; and the green digital numbers, glowing from the alarm clock, told me it was almost five o'clock. I flicked on the table lamp and reached for my gun laying on the night table beside the bed. I slowly walked to the door with the revolver pointed straight up, looked through the peephole, and saw T-Red pounding his fist on the door.

"Are you alone, Red?"

"No, I got the fucking Boston Symphony with me."

I unlatched the chain and turned the doorknob, then turned around and walked straight to the chair alongside the bed and plopped down in it. T-Red let himself in and stood on the other side of the bed gazing at my sleepy face and the gun resting in my lap.

"You know I don't like you coming here Red, and lately it's been a habit with you. This better be good."

"Good? My information is *numero uno*. How much scratch did you make on that horse last night?" he asked while he looked at the stack of money folded over and held together with a rubber band on my night table.

"Let's skip the commercial and get right to it."

T-Red sat on the edge of the bed and told me that the tip on the winning horse came from Frank Duplessis.

"That's not even his horse, Red."

"I know. I thought it was odd that he let me in on it because he doesn't share much information. But, hey. . . we take it where we can find it, right? Anyway, after the race Duplessis grabs me leaving the cashier's window in the grandstand and pulls me aside. He says I can return the favor and asked if I remembered that matter he discussed with me about The Gallop. He's kind of talking in code, you know, and real low. I could barely hear him above the crowd noise. So I nod yeah, and he says to come to his place this morning. This is it man, he wants to meet you."

"What did you tell him about me?"

"That you were connected, could get the job done, a pro. I told him he had already seen you with me that morning weeks ago at the bush track. Also, he better have plenty of cash if he was serious."

I was pleased the way T-Red handled the set-in. Duplessis wanted us to meet him at his training facility that morning, and after my change of clothes we headed out to a state road north of Evangeline Downs. T-Red was quieter than usual and I figured he was contemplating the end of his involvement with me. I told him to make the re-introduction to Duplessis brief and then cut out away from our conversation. T-Red pointed me onto a winding dirt road that cut through tall pines, cypress trees, and small low-lying areas with pools of standing water. The low areas were full of palmettos, whose evergreen fronds of spindly leaves gave lush green color to the swamp. We arrived at a large clearing, which was Duplessis' training center. Two long barns stood parallel to each other, constructed of gray cinder-block and covered with large tin roofs that hung over the shed-rows. The stalls faced the outside of the barns, and most of the horses stood with their heads sticking out above the lower half of the Dutch doors in each stall. We drove slowly to the end of the first barn and parked behind the building. I followed T-Red through the shed-row area, where white leg bandages that had been washed were strung across the railing to dry. The pungent smell of horse liniment lingered throughout the barn. There were fifteen or twenty horses stalled on either side of the building and the same amount in the parallel barn. I asked T-Red if Frank Duplessis owned that many horses.

"Nah. He has about a dozen for himself and trains the rest for owners in the oil and gas business here and in Texas. About half of these are babies being broken for the races."

Several young Cajun boys were atop horses coming to and from the half-mile training track in front of the barns. A half-dozen grooms, all black, tended to the horses as they came off the track from their workouts. There were two large cement pads where the grooms were bathing horses. We walked to a small tack room used as an office and T-Red stuck his head inside, but found it empty. He asked one of the grooms where we could find Duplessis and an elderly black man, small and thin with snow-white hair, answered back while pointing to the track. I noticed that all the black grooms and the Cajun riders spoke French to each other with the occasional English word or phrase mixed in.

We walked up a small incline to the track rail and stood on the wooden steps used for observation of the workouts on the bull-ring track. Directly in front of us was a two-horse starting gate used to train inexperienced horses, as well as to break veteran horses from the gate for timing their workouts. A beautiful young two-year-old filly was being led to the gate by an older rider. She was a light dappled gray color with an intelligent head and excellent conformation, and her build and color resembled more of the ultimate Arabian ancestry shared by all thoroughbreds. She looked all around in the curious manner of two-year-olds; and it was easy to tell she had not had much gate training up to this point. She was somewhat jittery as the rider urged her into the starting gate. Frank Duplessis stood behind the horse as she entered the gate, holding a large aluminum water syringe in his hand. When the filly was inside the gate stall, Duplessis quickly closed the rear door, locking horse and rider in the gate. He then lifted the horse's tail with one hand, and with the other took the one-hundred ml syringe with its six inch tube and shoved it forcefully into the horse's rectum. He injected the syringe with a quick blast. I could see the filly's eyes roll back for an instant, exposing the whites of her eyes. Her body muscles tightened and her ears pinned back at the same time. About a full second later, Duplessis released the front door of the starting gate and the bell rang, and the horse shot out of the gate like a rocket with the exercise rider holding on for dear life. Duplessis looked our way, laughing, with the large metal syringe dangling from his hand. After a quarter mile around the track, the rider gained control of the filly and galloped her back to the starting gate.

    The young horse was now covered in body sweat which turned her coat a dull, battleship gray color. There was a froth of kidney sweat between her hind legs and a trickle of reddish-orange liquid running down her legs from under her tail. As the rider urged the horse into the starting gate once again, Duplessis stuck the large syringe into a gallon glass jar of red liquid and pulled back the plunger, filling the syringe. When she was in the gate, Duplessis latched the rear and this time shoved the syringe into the horse's vagina and injected the red liquid. He waited a second, then released the front door and when the bell rang the filly again bolted out of the gate like lightning.

"What the hell is he doing, Red?"

"I thought you were a race-tracker, Tony. Frank is the best at training a young horse to break out of the gate quickly. That's Tabasco sauce in that syringe."

I had seen many strange things around race tracks, many different approaches, but this kind of cruelty ranked right up there with letting horses die from painful colic to collect insurance money and letting them run on fractured legs to collect a share of purse money. The hot Cajun concoction, produced only miles away at Avery Island and found in small bottles on every restaurant table in America, had found another, more perverse use. My face flushed with anger, then I suddenly remembered that this was out of character for a hit man. I did my best to put aside what I had seen. Duplessis walked towards the barn and motioned for us to follow him to his small office in the tack room. There was a grin on his face and he was pleased with the gray horse's reaction to his gate training method. Without turning his head toward us Duplessis said, "Wait till that bitch runs in the Louisiana Futurity this fall. She'll leave the gate faster than a quarter horse."

I watched as the elegant filly with distress in her eyes was led to the wash rack. Her ears twitched and her breathing was labored in short, heavy breaths. As soon as the rider un-tacked her, the old white-haired groom ran a hose with cool water down her back, then mercifully hosed out under her tail. As we finished the walk to Frank Duplessis' office I knew that I would never look at another bottle of Tabasco the same way.

In the office, T-Red spoke to Duplessis in French for a minute then said, "This is the Tony I told you about." He then turned around and without another word walked back out to the track, just as I had instructed. Frank Duplessis stuck out his hand to shake. I just stared at him for a moment and didn't reach back to him, which put him on the defensive. He frowned and lowered his lanky frame into a large, dilapidated chair that leaned to one side. He sat behind an old, small, cheap metal desk that looked like surplus from a government office.

I sat down on a bale of alfalfa that was stacked against the wall of the converted tack room. Leather bridles hung from large nails on all four walls and in one corner there were a couple of metal garbage cans with *Oats* crudely written on the covers. A thick layer of dust covered everything in the room.

"T-Red tells me you can be trusted and you're the man to do a job for me, is that true?"

"Depends on the job and how green your money is. Keep talking."

"I want somebody taken care of, I don't want to see them anymore. You know what I mean?"

"I know exactly what you mean. Before we go any further we need to get the money straight. You Coon-asses try to get by on the cheap with everything, and I'm sure this is no exception."

He didn't like the comment but took it in stride. I didn't mind pissing him off and needed him to dislike me. Since we were alone and I was not wearing a wire, anything he said would later have to be corroborated as evidence. I wanted to leave the particular details for a later meeting when our conversation could be recorded. However, I needed to cement a general deal of some sort now, or there might not be a future meeting.

"One guy. I want one guy taken out of the picture. What's the freight?"

"Twenty large. Ten up front, ten on the back end."

Duplessis rubbed his chin and stared at nothing in particular on his desk.

"That's a lot of money. What if I supply the equipment?"

"Like what?"

"Loaded pistol with a silencer."

He now had me mulling over the proposition. A silencer put him squarely in ATF jurisdiction, he could get up to ten years in a federal prison just for possessing a silencer. I knew we would also need the intelligence on who was making an assassination tool like a silencer. Murder itself and conspiracy to commit murder were state crimes, so with a silencer coming into play ATF had hard-core authority to keep the ball rolling in this case, no matter what the other agencies involved in the bank heist/murder in New Orleans wanted to do.

"Twenty thousand. That's the deal with or without the equipment. But I'll use what you supply if it's cool."

I wanted to seem indifferent about the gun and silencer. Too much eagerness about that aspect could tip him off to ATF presence. At this point I didn't know if he had access to a silencer or if he was on a fishing expedition about me.

"Ten up front?"

"That's the deal. I'll also need details from you on who, where, and when. I don't give a rat's ass about the *why*. Right now this whole conversation is bullshit until I see the cash."

"How do I know you won't rip me off for the front money?"

"You've already done your homework. Ritmo told me you've been asking questions and that he vouched for me. And if you didn't trust T-Red I wouldn't be here.

"Okay, so what's next?

"You can reach me at The Gallop when you've got the money."

"It'll be a few days. I'll have the information you asked for as well as the cash."

I stood up, leaned over Duplessis' desk and stared him in the face only inches away. "If any word gets back to me about what we discussed here, two things will happen. First, the deal is off. Second, look over your fucking shoulder because I might take you out for bringing heat on me."

"I understand. Don't worry, because I have a lot to lose if this goes bad. That won't happen."

His eyes looked down as I walked to the doorway. Before I got out of the small room he looked back up and said, "Twenty grand is a lot of money for one hit."

"Two hits, Frank."

"What do you mean?" he asked with a puzzled look.

"T-Red. I need to eliminate him after the job, maybe before - since he's the only one besides us who knows about this issue."

The coldness in his face warmed a little. For just a second he seemed worried, even concerned. He hadn't thought about anybody else being killed, and he had no reason for T-Red to die other than the fact that he had put Duplessis and I together. But the hesitation in his face quickly disappeared and the cold resolve returned as he said, "Whatever it takes. I'll be in touch."

I stepped into the shed-row and called for T-Red. Duplessis gazed at him with a lingering look. He now knew that T-Red was a man whose days were numbered. As we walked to the car I saw Duplessis watching me, and I could read his thoughts about how I would kill this unintended victim, a man I was pals with, just because it was part of my business. It clearly registered on the horse trainer's face that he was sold.

CHAPTER 17

Every day since I was on the ground Lyle Melancon supervised a squad of ATF agents working behind the scenes. They ran the names, addresses, and license plates listed in the notes I dropped for Lyle. They did the leg work on criminal background checks, and identified people and places from public records and files maintained by police agencies. They checked with our network of informants and scoured the daily newspapers in a multi-state area for any news of unsolved murders or contracts. For all we knew, the hit could have been set up in Louisiana to be carried out anywhere in the country – or outside the country for that matter. We had our fingers crossed constantly that no bodies turned up before I could work myself in to take the contract. Since my meeting with Frank Duplessis we could all breathe a little easier. I was convinced that he wanted me to do the job. But there was no guarantee that he hadn't already talked to someone else or hired more than one killer to make sure his murder scheme succeeded. The possibility was remote but couldn't be overlooked.

In addition to support agents in the field, the special operations division in Washington was monitoring the case, and I knew the cost of the operation was climbing. I wasn't surprised at the news Lyle gave me when I phoned him about the setup with Duplessis.

"We're underway, big boy."

"Thank Christ. How did it go?" Lyle asked.

"He'll be back to me soon. No details yet on the intended victim, but we set up the terms. This guy means business."

"The ivory tower is breathing down our necks, Tony. I don't know if they're antsy about the cost, or the pressure from the FBI and the New Orleans Police Department, or a combination of both. McKinney and the boys want to meet with you."

"Tell me this is a joke, Lyle. I'm up to my ass right now."

"I wish it was. They're on their way to New Orleans and want to meet with you in the next couple of days, as soon as you can work yourself away."

"Let's do it tomorrow and get it over with. I can't be gone long because the deal is too hot. I'll drive in and be there for eight o'clock. That'll spoil their government-paid vacation to New Orleans and cut it short. Those guys never come to the field when the case is in Bumfuck, Alaska."

"I'll be there too. And Tony, clean yourself up before you come."

That night The Gallop was hot. It was as crowded as I had ever seen. The blues band had their volume cranked up over the noise level of the crowd. T-Red sat on a stool slumped over the bar and was half lit. I sat next to him. He turned slowly towards me, said nothing, then looked straight ahead at the mirror behind the bar. I had never seen him drunk before, but he was on his way. He wasn't happy to see me and I sensed hostility. I leaned over and had to shout into his ear because of the noise.

"What's the word, Red?" He didn't answer. I tried again.

"Okay, spill it. Let's hear the bitch-and-gripe session."

He leaned back towards me and shouted in my ear. The conversation took place with us talking inches from each other's ears, bobbing back and forth so we could be heard, but not overheard by others. "We left Frank's place and all you talked about was bullshit. You didn't let me in on what happened with him, and this morning at the track he acted strange around me. I'm stuck in the middle not knowing shit, and I want out."

"*Pazienza,* Red. You've wanted out since day one. And you're not in the middle – you're one of the good guys for the first time in your cheesy life. I don't have time to explain now. Just avoid Frank."

I felt a small arm reach around my left side, across my chest, and with surprising accuracy a hand pinched my right nipple through my shirt. I flinched from the teasing pain and turned around to see Cheri standing behind me grinning. She asked, "Do you two want a private booth? Looks like you two are kissing."

I laughed but T-Red didn't. In a slow, liquored voice he said, "Screw you, bitch."

Cheri and I were both surprised because he usually joined in the teasing. "Is he drunk? He likes his brew, but I've never heard that tone out of him," Cheri said.

"He's halfway there," I said while rubbing the nipple that still smarted. "Be sure he doesn't get any more to drink or you'll have to take him home."

Ritmo walked in and went straight to work behind the bar as Cheri returned to waiting tables. I motioned him over and he leaned over the bar a few inches from me. I told him I'd be gone for a day or two, and to let Frank Duplessis know that if he asked for me.

"I know he pumped you about me, Ritmo."

"Yeah and I gave you the okay, Tony. So did Cliff. I don't want to know what that's about. Look . . ."

"You won't," I interrupted. "And I know what you're going to ask. When I get back I'll be in a position to deal with Cliff. I'm going out of town to line up some finances."

Ritmo nodded with a pleased look. "Can I tell Cliff?"

"Whatever makes you happy."

"*This* makes me happy, Tony." Ritmo lifted his beefy hand from under the bar and drew a small marijuana cigarette to his lips. He took a deep breath from the joint and stuck his arm across to bar for me to take it. I had smelled weed in the place before, but up to now Ritmo had been cooler than this. The move was unexpected and I had only a split-second to react. I grabbed the joint from him and took a long, deep hit from the thin hand-rolled joint. I held the smoke in my lungs for several seconds and felt the fuzzy bee stings inside. I gave my best imitation of a pot smoker and exhaled slowly while handing the joint back to Ritmo. He took another hit, then threw the roach down and stomped it like a regular cigarette butt and got back to work.

The weed incident was another reminder of the little things that can sabotage an undercover role. If I refused the joint I would need a plausible excuse, and have only a second to come up with one. And that would only stave off the problem until the next time the situation came up. I took the hit to get it behind me. I could now make excuses in the future with little fear of suspicion. The incident also brought me into focus about my relationship with Cheri. I had made a series of excuses about why I hadn't dated her and it was wearing thin. Nobody thought I didn't have interest in women, but if I didn't pursue her, some people might wonder. The last thing I needed was people wondering about me. She walked past me on her way to the tables and I stood in front of her, blocking her way. I took her drink tray and placed it on the bar. I grabbed both her hands with mine, gave her a peck on the cheek and told her that when I returned in a few days I would take her to dinner. Her face brightened. She bounced up on her toes a couple of times, then grabbed her tray and walked away to the tables. Without breaking her stride she turned her head around to me and shouted, "It's a date."

    I grabbed T-Red under the elbow and lifted him off the barstool. I reached in his pocket for his keys, then walked him out to his pickup truck and shoved him into the seat. "Go to sleep, Red. When you wake up Ritmo will have your keys." I didn't want him driving in that condition, but more importantly I didn't want any of his drunken words to be about me in The Gallop.

CHAPTER 18

I sat at the small table in my room and tried to prepare for whatever the meeting with the ATF brass in just a few hours would bring. I shrugged off the notion that they were coming to New Orleans just to party on Bourbon Street. I knew there was something important involved beyond the serious matters at hand. Trying to sleep was useless so I decided to make the trip early. The two-hour drive was tense. My mind wandered, trying to figure out if I was on the carpet. Some of my expenses were unorthodox but not illegal, and besides, the bosses dealt with creative writing on expense reports every day. I usually covered my ass well from training and instinct, but there was always the possibility of something that wasn't done by the book that could come back to haunt me.

Upon arrival in the city, I enjoyed again seeing some of the familiar landmarks. I drove past the cities of the dead, the unique cemeteries where people are buried above ground in small house tombs or mausoleums. I saw the tourists and their guides, familiar sights in these cemeteries. The French who colonized and ruled New Orleans in the eighteenth century, learned so many years ago that the shallow water levels of a city situated below sea level necessitated the novel gravesites. Normal underground burial resulted in the coffins literally popping up out of the ground after a hard rain, so they devised the raised tombs that are still used. In France only royalty and the wealthy were buried in such ornate tombs, but here the paupers and rich were all afforded the same elaborate resting places.

I arrived downtown around six-thirty. The morning rush hour traffic had not arrived. The federal building wasn't open yet so I parked the Camaro in a metered space and took what I thought would be a short nap. An hour later there was loud, rapid tapping on the car window my head was resting against. I looked up to see a large, round, ebony face peering at me only inches away from the other side of the glass. His head was covered with a uniform police hat with a silver frontispiece bearing the word *Patrolman*. He tapped loudly with his nightstick until I rolled down the window.

"I'm okay, officer."

"Is that so? Get out!" he ordered.

I stood outside the car as the morning traffic hustled by. The cop was alone and there was no police car nearby. He was huge, built like an NFL player and he towered over me. He wore the familiar dark blue uniform pants and light blue starched shirt that I had worn on the NOPD. Above his silver star-and-crescent badge were several service medals and the hash marks on his sleeves told me he had at least sixteen years on the job. He reached into the car and retrieved my coat, which was lying on the seat. He removed the identification from the wallet, and turned his head toward the radio mike that was clipped to the epaulet of his shirt. He called in the codes along with my name and car information for record checks. A female voice came right back over his radio and read a list of arrests for Anthony Parrino.

His eyebrows raised, and he made me assume the routine spread-eagle position against the hood of the car. He kicked my legs out to a stretch so far that I was almost horizontal. He patted me down for weapons and found six hundred dollars in my hip pocket. He folded the money and put it in his shirt pocket. "You mind if I search your car?" he said, more in the manner of a statement than a question.

We both knew he had no warrant, but the slightest permission gave him authority to take the car apart. I couldn't afford the complications of his finding my firearm under the front seat. The radio check told him I was a convicted felon and the gun would put me under arrest. How nice for me to be in the slammer while the ATF bosses waited for me to show up for the meeting. I gambled that his being a veteran would stop him from overreacting, and I replied, "Fuck you."

By now, a small crowd of onlookers gathered, most of them on their way to work. I winced when the officer put the end of his nightstick squarely in the middle of my back. I started to say something when I noticed a husky figure wearing a tan suit approach the cop. I stretched my neck from the spread position to see Lyle flashing his badge. They talked quietly for a minute, then Lyle grabbed me by the arm and pulled me to the sidewalk. The seasoned cop looked hard at me, then dug into his shirt pocket for the cash and stuck it in Lyle's hand. He walked away slowly, both hands clutching the ends of his nightstick behind his back. He swaggered a few steps in the manner of foot patrol cops, then turned his head toward us and barked to Lyle, "Keep his sorry ass off my beat."

Lyle locked my car and whisked me off into a coffee shop in the next block. "You come back to the big city for one day and get rousted? Maybe you've been in Acadiana too long."

"How did you keep my cover with that cop?"

"I told him we busted you last week and you were appearing in court this morning and we wanted to question you. I think he only half-assed bought it, but since I took responsibility he's got better things to do. By the way, didn't I tell you to get cleaned up?

"I did."

Lyle laughed. "You look like a stone criminal. And you should have stood a little closer to your razor."

We walked to the federal building and I realized what Lyle meant as we rode the elevator with government employees dressed in their typical button-down office attire. My ultra-suede sport coat and Bally shoes didn't fit in with the gray flannel suits. When we arrived on the ATF floor, Lyle guided me to a rear conference room away from the general offices. Seated at a thirty-foot mahogany table were Paul McKinney, Jim Fenton, and Jim King. King was the special agent in charge of the New Orleans office so he was responsible for anything going in his territory, but I knew this show was McKinney's. I was always glad to see Jim Fenton, and welcomed the humor he usually added to things.

We shook hands all around and got down to business right away. McKinney led the meeting. He had a dour look on his face. I knew of his reputation as a stand-up guy but also a company man, so at first his demeanor didn't signal anything unusual. Jim Fenton packed a fresh wad of scented tobacco into his pipe, held a lighter over the bowl, and drew several strong puffs. He listened with the rest of us as McKinney spoke.

"The FBI and NOPD have turned up the heat on us. Interpol wants to know if we're in possession of those bank notes. They're all threatening to go to the Director's level if we don't give them something soon. The bank robbery and cop killing we came across as a sidelight to our investigation is a top priority for them. We can keep the NOPD at arm's length a while longer, but if the FBI pushes we could have a pissing match between the Departments of Justice and Treasury." McKinney paused for some kind of reply from me.

"What's new about that?"

McKinney raised his voice and said, "Here's what's new about it. It's not going to happen on my watch."

"I know that's important, but we're already aware. And you're not here to debrief me since we're still on the ground. So why did you really bring me here?"

There was silence from everyone. I looked at Lyle and he shrugged, as if he was just as puzzled as I was. Fenton puffed on his pipe and Jim King squirmed a little in his chair. McKinney reached into his briefcase which was sitting on the floor.

"We got this through legal channels and it's our duty to serve it on you." He handed me several legal sized sheets of paper. My eyes went immediately to the citation in the upper left-hand corner:

State of Florida
Dade County
Gina DiMarco Palumbo vs. August Palumbo
Petition for Divorce

Of all the reasons I may have imagined for the meeting, this was the last I expected. I didn't read past the citation. My eyes bugged. Rage and confusion swept over me. I jumped up from my chair and clenched the conference table. I felt like I was in a time warp, in another place. I pounded my fist on the table so hard that the men seated around it flinched. I was hurt and mostly angered at the same time. Anger at Gina, anger at ATF, and unexpected, uncontrollable anger at Lyle Melancon. He was my contact agent, the personal representative to my family. Even though he had never met them he was my surrogate for anything they needed. Surely he knew this was in the works. He must have known, but kept it from me.

Lyle, who was seated next to me, leaned over to look at the legal papers. My anger exploded. I swung my body towards him and from a leveraged position hit him square on the chin with a strong right hand. He was like a boxer leaning into the punch and his large frame toppled on to Jim Fenton who was seated next to him. Fenton's pipe and its contents flew out of his hand and skidded across the waxed floor. Jim King lurched from his chair and grabbed my arms from behind, to keep me from Lyle, whose chin was split wide open. Phil McKinney pressed a handkerchief over Lyle's lower face and it filled with blood.

McKinney and King pushed me back down into a chair. King motioned Lyle out of the room and everyone else got back to their seats. Nobody spoke for a minute or so. I breathed heavy and my heart raced. I picked up the legal papers and studied them more closely. Gina had filed the papers three weeks earlier.

"Why did you wait so Goddamned long to tell me?"

Jim Fenton spoke up. "First of all, Tony, Lyle Melancon knew nothing about this until today, I assure you."

"He's my contact with Gina. He had to know."

"That's between you and Lyle. But he didn't find out from us. Nobody did. Our office in Washington did get it ten days ago. We had arguments about when to notify you, and decided that a little more time in the cold might nail down Duplessis and the other things you have going."

"You didn't want to piss off the FBI so you left me out there in the dark like the village idiot, not knowing that my wife had filed for divorce. What kind of balls does this outfit have?"

McKinney's countenance grew angry for just a second. "It was my call, Tony. This case is no chicken-shit sting operation. We've got a lot invested and lives at stake, including yours. The deed was already done as far as the divorce being filed. What you didn't know couldn't hurt you or interfere in a way to jeopardize your life..."

"Or *your* fucking investigation," I scowled. I knew that I needed to talk to Gina immediately, to find out what happened, to square things away. "I'm getting on the next plane to Miami."

"We've already got your ticket for this afternoon's flight. But there's more."

"More?"

McKinney took a deep breath and looked over at Fenton and King. He then turned to look me in the eye. "The return flight on that ticket is tomorrow afternoon."

"Twenty-four hours to fix a marriage? Is this a sick joke?"

"Look, Tony. Bureau policy is not to force any agent into an undercover situation. You can bail if you want, but you can't be replaced, it won't work. If you don't continue we'll have to shut it down. Four months down the tubes. Duplessis will find another hit man, whoever is out there making silencers will stay in business, the FBI will be on their own with the bank job, and the NOPD will have to settle for our leads to find their own cop killers. We'll fade the heat. Do what you have to do in Miami, but if you're not on that return flight tomorrow we're pulling the plug." McKinney did a masterful job of putting me on a guilt trip. Then they all slouched back in their chairs and gave me a sympathetic look, putting the ball in my court. We sat and stared at each other for several minutes. McKinney and King had been in similar circumstances. Fenton was a lawyer by training with no undercover background himself, and I sensed that he had come to the meeting mostly because of his affinity for me. I appreciated that, as well as his legal advice on how and when to answer the divorce petition, in the event I couldn't get the situation straightened out. He finally found a place for a weak joke and said, "Remember, this legal advice is worth exactly what you pay for it."

A rookie agent drove me to the airport. We didn't speak along the way. I studied his crisp, clean shirt surrounded by a well-cut suit and his polished shoes. He also studied me, glancing over several times, and probably wondered what in hell I was involved in and where I was going.

CHAPTER 19

Because of flight delays it was almost dark when I arrived in Miami. Since I had no luggage, I made my way quickly through the travelers that milled, sat, or slept on the floor of the crowded gate areas. I grabbed a rental car and made the usual twenty-five minute drive to my house in less than fifteen.

An old Volkswagen Beetle that I didn't recognize was parked in the driveway. Apprehension turned to anger when my keys didn't fit the front door locks. I knocked quietly on the door, and noticed someone peeking out at me through a front window curtain. There was no answer so I knocked louder. I heard the security chain slide inside the door before it opened. A teenage girl's face appeared through the small opening.

"Can I help you?" she asked.

"Where's Gina?"

"At the market. I'm babysitting."

"What's your name?"

"Shannon."

"Well, Shannon, I live here. Let me in."

"Gina told me not to let anyone in."

My first reaction was to push the door in, but that would only aggravate the situation. I didn't want to frighten the girl or make a scene. I showed her my driver's license I.D. through the door.

"You don't know me Shannon, but I'm Mr. Palumbo. I've been away on a trip. It's okay to let me in."

"Your driver's license says your name is Parrino."

"Shit. Wait a minute, please don't close the door."

The girl was puzzled, and I went back to the rental car and got my ATF badge and credentials. I showed them to her and she hesitated for a moment, then closed the door. I was planning my next move when the chain slid again, and the door opened.

Once inside, I went to Nick's room and found him asleep. I joined Shannon in the living room and sat on the couch. I felt awkward, like a stranger in my own house. There were several pieces of new furniture I didn't recognize. After a few minutes of quiet conversation with the babysitter, the front door opened and Gina appeared with grocery bags under her arms. I stood up to help her, and her face went pale.

"Shannon! Didn't I tell you not to let anyone in?"

The teenager became upset and tried to find a reply. "Well, he . . ."

"Don't blame the kid, Gina. How much do you owe her?"

"Ten dollars."

The petite girl grabbed up a few textbooks and her purse that were on the coffee table and shuffled to the door. I gave her a twenty and she made a quick exit.

"Did you sweet talk her or bully your way in?"

"Neither. I live here."

"Not anymore. Didn't you get the papers?"

"Of course, that's why I'm here. What in hell is this all about?"

"My lawyer said Washington received those papers weeks ago, and you're here now?" She stopped and thought for a moment, then said, "Why am I not surprised, as far down as we are on your priority list."

"I just got them this morning. I have people for you to call if you want proof."

Her voice grew louder as she spoke. "Don't bother. I've had it, Tony. We don't have a life together.

"I haven't seen you for months, haven't even spoken to you except for a few minutes at a time. Six months before that you lived out of a suitcase God knows where or on some Secret Service detail. I don't know if you're dead or alive, well or sick, or even where you are. What kind of marriage is that? What kind of bullshit life is it? Your son is growing up without you, and we've had to make a life for ourselves."

"I don't get it. A few weeks ago you seemed fine on the phone, even upbeat. What happened?"

"The papers were filed before that conversation. I was relieved, on something of a high, knowing that I was taking control for a change. Besides, there was no sense in upsetting you since you couldn't do anything about it. I figured ATF would hold those papers away from you for a while, maybe until the case was finished. I was right."

"Wrong. It's not finished . . . unless I don't go back." I looked directly into Gina's face and promised to stay home. I told her I had lots of leave time accumulated and I'd spend it all at home, and to hell with the job. Gina rolled her eyes. We both knew it was a half-hearted gesture and the idea was dismissed. She folded her arms and her eyes hardened. I was surprised by her question.

"Who are you screwing, Tony?"

"What kind of question is that?"

"You're gone this long, I'm sure you're doing it to somebody unless you're tying it in a knot."

I sat on the couch, buried my face in my hands and collected my thoughts. I hadn't been unfaithful to her except for the teasing and flirting with Cheri, and the occasional pinch on the behind I delivered to the cocktail waitresses at the track. The idea of explaining this to Gina quickly passed.

"Look, there's nobody. I could ask you the same question."

Wrong move. Her face reddened and she reached over for the closest thing near her, which was a grocery bag. She grabbed a large bunch of shallots held together with a small red rubber band and dashed over to where I was sitting. She lunged on top of me with her knees digging into the top of my thighs and raised the shallots high with her arm, landing them squarely on top of my head. She repeated the thrashing several times as I covered up with my arms. Each time she came down, a spray of wet green onions landed on my head as she shouted in cadence, "You son-of-a-bitch! son-of-a-bitch! son-of-a-bitch!, landing one stroke with each syllable.

"Wait! Hold up!" I shouted just as the rubber band snapped and her baton of shallots finally fell apart. Green, frayed stalks were scattered all over me, the couch, and the floor.

"I had no right to say that, I'm sorry. Look, this whole thing is crazy." Next, I tried the heavy artillery.

"We're Catholic, we're Italian. Divorce goes against the things we believe in."

She was slightly out of breath and leaned her body on me. We said nothing for a while, then I heard Nick jostling around in his room. The argument had wakened him. He ran from his room and jumped up on both of us, spread his arms and legs, and held on tight. I enjoyed the momentary group hug but was mostly taken by surprise when he ran into the room. The last I remembered, he was merely toddling, unsure of his steps. Gina was right, he was growing up without me.

I helped clean up, then played with Nick. Gina gave me the silent treatment but acted civil in front of our son. We all sat down to a meal she hastily prepared, and after dinner I walked Nick around the block and carried him on my shoulders. We watched television for a while, then I bathed him and read him to sleep from one of the many story books I had mailed home for him. These were the things I missed so much. The house seemed especially quiet and I tried to break the ice.

"You're losing your touch, Gina. Last time you beat me on the head it was with a shoe. Now you're down to flogging me with veggies."

She managed a slight smile and said, "That was a long time ago. I'm out of practice."

We sat down across the kitchen table from each other. She somehow seemed older than I remembered. Stress had made its mark on her face. Her hair and clothes were not as neat as usual. What could I say to fix things? Would pleading do any good, or simply prolong the inevitable?

"Gina, we both love each other, don't we? Then you can't go through with this."

She gave me an icy glare. "Watch me," she said. "We need a husband and father around here, not some phantom. Nick doesn't know if you're real or some imaginary figure from one of his books." She squared her shoulders and became businesslike. "This wasn't a whim, Tony. And, it's not just this case. There will always be another case, another emergency, another assignment you can't tell me anything about. Go back to your case, to what's important to you."

I was crushed. She had made up her mind, and any further argument was useless. She wouldn't let me touch her or get close. I fell asleep on the couch and was awakened at nine o'clock the next morning by the sound of Nick running around in circles next to me. I tried several times to start up a conversation with Gina, but all I got from her was a cold stare and silence. I prepared to leave and gave Nick an extra hug as Gina hustled me to the front door. I made a final plea for her to drop the divorce proceedings, then left. Nick stood near the front door waving as I drove away.

By the time I reached the airport, there was only four minutes to flight time. I ran to the ticket counter and broke in front of a long line of passengers waiting to check in. I showed my badge to the ticket agent, a middle-aged woman neatly attired in her Eastern Airlines smock, and explained that I had to be on the flight to New Orleans that was leaving the gate. She immediately picked up the phone and made contact with the flight tower.

"They're holding the flight for five minutes. Gate forty-one. You'd better hurry."

I ran down the concourse onto the jetway and 'badged' the flight attendant standing in the doorway of the plane. I made the way to my seat and plopped down. As we taxied onto the airfield, I felt the familiar captivity of being in a large tube. I was depressed by the failure of my visit home. I resigned myself to put the family matters aside and get on with the task of completing the undercover assignment. I harbored a faint hope that after finishing things up I could put my personal life back together. From the window, the trees, cars, and buildings, now miniature size, looked as if they were in a diorama. I took off my coat, and two small pieces of green onions fell from the pocket. I didn't know whether to laugh or cry.

Assassin Hunter

CHAPTER 20

I expected the customary rookie agent to pick me up at the gate when I deplaned in New Orleans. Instead, I found Lyle leaning against a wall with his arms folded. There was a straight red line under his chin, held together with several black stitches. He said nothing as I extended my hand to him. He didn't hesitate and gripped it tightly.

"Gina told me you knew nothing about it. I'm sorry I clipped you."

Lyle pointed to the catgut knots sticking out of his chin and said, "Lucky punch." Then he asked about Gina.

"It doesn't look good. I did everything but beg."

Lyle was sympathetic, but thought the same way I did. Block it out. Concentrate on the case, get it done, then maybe I could try to salvage what was left of my personal life. We talked on the way downtown to pick up my car.

"The boys will be pleased you were on that flight. They wanted me to notify them immediately if you weren't on it.

Their asses are biting button holes waiting to find out. Let 'em sweat a little longer."

Three messages were waiting for me at the Plantation. Two were from T-Red, one from Ritmo Angelle. I got T-Red on the phone.

"Glad you caught me, Tony, I'm on my way to the track. Have you talked to Ritmo? He's trying to reach you in a big way, asked me to bird-dog you."

"I'll get hold of him."

"By the way, Frank Duplessis is still giving me the chill. That asshole makes me uneasy."

"Good, Red. Maybe it'll keep you on your toes."

I drove to The Gallop since it was almost time for Ritmo's shift. He was already there behind the bar, but dressed in a loud, plaid sport jacket instead of his bar outfit. His toupee was squarely on his head and he had an aroma of cheap aftershave.

"Where you been, Dago?"

"Damn, Ritmo, I was only gone two days. What's the issue?"

"Money. Cliff wants us to meet him about that deal. He'll be at the cock fights tonight. Also, Frank Duplessis has been in here looking for you. That guy never comes in here alone, usually he's with his horse owners. He thinks he's too good for the place. But he's been here twice looking for you. He's creepy."

I laughed at Ritmo calling anyone else creepy. He poured us both a drink and I asked him about the cock fights, which I had never seen.

"Let's go. We might make some extra scratch tonight."Ritmo and I got into his dated, dark brown Lincoln and headed to a little town named Scott outside of Lafayette. It was a particularly dark night. As we drove along the highway the smooth ride of the big car and baritone hum of the defective muffler almost put me to sleep. The news report on the radio announced that California governor Ronald Reagan, the long-shot candidate to wrestle the Republican nomination from Gerald Ford, would make a campaign swing through Louisiana. He was giving a campaign speech at a fundraiser in Lafayette the following weekend.

"Not many presidential candidates come to the bayou," Ritmo cracked. "Half the town will show up, even Democrats will show. Cops will be working overtime and they'll be bunched near the speech at the college. It wouldn't be a bad time to pull a score on the other side of town while the heat is all tied up."

"Think so, Ritmo? What about all those fucking feds that will be crawling all over the place? And I'm sure the state police will be in force. You could bump into them by accident they'll be so many. Bad idea."

"I hadn't thought of that, Tony. I guess you were a step ahead of me."

The big car turned slowly onto a narrow oyster shell road that cut through a large swamp. The road was only wide enough for one vehicle. I wondered what happened when a car exiting the road approached one coming in. The answer was, there was no quick exit. The road wound for about two miles into the woods and I could hear and feel the oyster shells crunch beneath the car tires. We came to the end of the road where there was a large, tall structure that looked like an old barn. It was made of wide, unpainted cypress planks. Slivers of light slipped through the cracks between the boards and the wide door, which gave off the only light in a pitch-black area.

There were at least a hundred vehicles, mostly pickup trucks, parked all around the building. The sound of frogs and crickets filled the swamp. As Ritmo parked, his headlights illuminated an old pickup truck with a half dozen wire cages in the bed, each containing a rooster. Two men stood behind the truck unloading the cages, and I recognized one of them as old Comeaux, the horse trainer. Before we got out of the car Ritmo told me to leave my gun because we would be checked for weapons. I placed my .38 snub-nose under the front seat. We approached Comeaux and the other man and Ritmo gave them a greeting in French. I shook hands with Comeaux and asked about his old horse, Bob's Dream.

"A bowed tendon forced me to turn him out to pasture for a while. The old boy knows when he needs a rest so he goes lame on me. But you can cash a bet on this red chicken tonight. He's small, but he's hell on wheels."

We left the men at the truck and Ritmo led us to the front door. He knocked, and a slat on the door slid open. A pair of dark eyes appeared on the other side and looked back and forth at Ritmo and me before the door was opened. We walked into a closet-sized room, and there was another door in front of us. The young Cajun who let us in then locked the door we came through. The three of us were locked between two doors in the tiny room. The sentry had a large, .44 caliber magnum revolver, a *Dirty Harry* weapon, stuck in the front of his waistband. He patted us down for weapons and, satisfied that we had none, opened the door to the main building. I knew the checkpoint wasn't so much to keep the cops out, but to prevent any bust-out bandits from jacking the men inside and robbing them of the sums of cash they were holding.

The inside of the old barn was like no structure I had been in before. It was built entirely of heavy cypress planks. Bare light bulbs hung from the rafters and lit the place with a rather dim yellow glow. There were tiered sections of spectator stands where men stood, talking and haggling in French over the contestants in the next cock fight. The standing-only sections were built like an amphitheater in circular fashion, and the center of the building was a large dirt floor used as a fighting pit. The room was filled with smoke and a thick haze hung in the rafters, adding to the dim atmosphere. Most of the men clutched stacks of cash in their hands.

Five house men stood in a large circle on the edges of the dirt arena, facing the crowd. They held up large wads of cash and fingers to indicate the odds the house was laying on each bird. When a bettor accepted the odds they took his cash and wrote out a receipt on a small brown piece of paper. The Cajuns in the stands shot fingers back at the odds-makers, and the whole scene reminded me of a crude stock exchange or commodities pit. Some of the spectators wagered with each other if they negotiated better odds than the house men offered. The entire procedure was a throwback to the days before pari-mutuel betting at racetracks, when bookmakers operated the legal betting and set the odds.

Lined up on the floor on opposite sides of the arena was a number of wire cages containing roosters of all sizes and breeds. A small roar erupted from the crowd when a tall, burly man wearing worn denim overalls brought two cages to the center of the floor. He placed the cages about a yard apart, and the men yelled and furiously waved their fists full of cash. One cage contained a small, reddish-brown rooster with black on the end of his feathers. He had a large spot below his neck where no feathers grew because of scar material, and a talon was missing on one of his feet. The other cage held a snow white rooster, highlighted by the red of his eyes and crown and the yellow of his talons. The yelling peaked when the burly man took the brown rooster from his cage and held the bird over his head, turning in all directions so each section of the crowded building could get a good look. Then a smaller man with a scraggly salt-and-pepper beard, wearing a floppy straw hat, took the white rooster from his cage and did the same thing.

Ritmo pointed at one of the house men. He walked up to us and pulled out a brown betting slip. Ritmo handed him two one-hundred dollar bills and the man quickly scribbled on the paper with a stubby pencil and stuck it in Ritmo's hand.

"What's the action, Ritmo?"

"Gotta lay two to one on the brown bird, but he's a pro, been around a while. You get two to one for your sugar if you like the white one, but he's a rookie."

The house man booking Ritmo's bet looked hard at me, poking his fist full of cash in my direction and shouted,

"*Rouge o blanche?*

"He's motioning for you to get your money out and bet," Ritmo explained. " Ignore him and he'll go away and find another bettor."

The room was now quite warm and damp from the humidity of the swamp and from so many men being closed up in it. I took off my coat and noticed sweat beads forming on Ritmo's forehead just under the edge of his toupee. Why he even wore that rug to a place like this was amusing to me. We both began to perspire through our shirts, as did most of the others.

The two men holding the roosters walked to opposite sides of the arena and turned to face each other. They affixed sharp, stainless steel blades to the talons of their respective roosters. The blades were double-edged and about four inches long. Then, as in an old-fashioned duel, the men slowly walked toward each other in the center. They thrust the roosters toward each other then quickly pulled them back, taunting and teasing them. They repeated this several times until the birds could barely be held back any more. Suddenly, they threw them both down in the dirt toward each other and backed away.

The birds wasted no time in pecking and jumping at each other. The crowd shouted loudly as in a boxing match, and cheered on their favorite with each blow delivered. The birds pecked and clawed at each other in close quarters for several minutes. The white rooster, somewhat bigger than his foe, seemed to establish himself early with a couple of strong leaps on his smaller opponent. He spread his large wings and crowed loudly each time he jumped. He knocked the reddish-brown bird to the dirt, and a few brown feathers shook loose from his body and floated in the air. The weight of the white bird seemed to surprise and overpower the brown one. The smaller bird paused, like a fighter getting up off the canvas after a knockdown. The hackles raised around his neck, and he leaped several feet into the air and came down with his bladed talon on top of the other rooster in a stomping motion, driving the double edged blade through the white wing. Severely stunned, the white bird hobbled a short distance, then launched a flying attack of his own, jumping feet first. He clawed at the smaller bird but his blade barely made contact. He used his larger beak to bite at the brown rooster's neck. The panic screeching from the birds was now quite severe.

They pecked and clawed at each other fiercely, and white and brown-black feathers were thrust into the air as they fought. Trickles of blood began to appear on the white rooster as they continued, but it was hard to tell whose blood it was. As each bird received more cuts and blows, they seemed to get more enraged and more oblivious to their injuries. It became obvious that the contest could only end with the death of one or both of the combatants.

There was a brief pause in the action, as if it was a planned timeout. The birds backed off and gave each other a fixed look. They breathed heavily. Suddenly, the brown bird jumped in the air and flapped his wings violently as if using a diversionary tactic. He then dropped on the white rooster with a forceful thrust, and the razor-sharp blade cut him deeply in the chest just below the throat. A large amount of blood now streamed from the wound and the entire chest area of the white bird was stained in red. He fell to one side, gasping for breath. Blood pooled in the hole where one of his eyes had been. His beak was split and broken on the end. As the brown rooster sensed a kill, he was relentless in his attack. The white bird tried to rally each time the red rooster charged, but he was hurt too badly to avoid the eventual outcome. Although the match was decided at this point, the men in the arena allowed it to continue until the smaller rooster finally broke his defenseless opponent's neck with a savage thrust. The white bird's body went limp, but his heart, which was now protruding from the deep, wide cut in his chest, was still beating outside his body.

The crowd, most of whom bet on the favorite, cheered and held up their brown paper slips, waiting for the house men to pay them off. As the noise subsided, the burly man in overalls picked up the exhausted brown rooster, held him up and turned around to the crowd as he had done before the fight. He then returned him to his cage. The bearded Cajun in the straw hat walked over to the bloodied and broken bird. I was touched as he knelt over the rooster, then realized he was only untying the blade from his talon for future use. He then scooped up the bird from the dirt with a shovel, walked over to a large garbage can, and with blood running off the end of the bird's white wings, unceremoniously dumped the carcass into the can. The smell of death was now added to the dank arena.

Assassin Hunter

CHAPTER 21

Cliff Dubroc stood out in the crowd of men who were dressed mostly in denim and khaki work clothes. He was sharp in pressed slacks and a heavily starched white shirt. His gold rings and Rolex watch rounded out his appearance. Two taller, more casually dressed men followed him around. He walked towards us counting a coarse fan of one-hundred dollar bills, followed by his two shadows.

"You guys bet the winner?" Cliff was bragging more than asking a question. Ritmo nodded and grinned. Cliff then put the money into his pocket, grabbed me by the elbow, and walked me aside. "We have some unfinished business. You still interested in those notes?"

"If you still have them and the price is right."

The crowd noise grew loud again as another pair of roosters were taken out of their cages.

Dubroc was smart. He got me there to talk about the deal, in the middle of the noisy place, in case I was wearing a hidden microphone.

He knew that tapes or transmissions made over a wire were generally unintelligible in the backdrop of crowd noise. Defense attorneys have red-letter days when tapes are offered as evidence and played before juries. Cautious criminals had led me near loud jukeboxes in past situations in order to equalize the effect of wires. Cliff's genius was that any discussion taped that night couldn't be used. Even if we didn't cut the deal and no transaction took place, the garbled tape precluded him from prosecution on a conspiracy charge. But his precaution was needless since I wasn't wearing a mike.

"Here's the deal, Tony. Two bits on the dollar. That's half price from our original discussion."

"Twenty cents. That's my last offer. But to sweeten the pot, I'll take all you have." He rubbed his chin as if he was making a tough decision, but we both knew we had struck a fair price.

"Done. . . if you can do it in forty-eight hours. Thursday night in my office."

During the entire drive back from the swamp, Ritmo cited one scenario after another about how to use the Reagan visit as an advantage to pull a score. He was like a dog with a bone. Each time he brought it up, I answered with a reason why his plan wouldn't work. I hoped to convince him. "Ritmo, you might as well just walk into the police station and turn yourself in." He finally dropped the matter, but I could see that the wheels still turned in his head.

I contacted Lyle right away and told him about the deal with Cliff. We kicked around the idea of getting a search warrant for his office in The Gallop, but decided against it. First, we had less than two days to secure a warrant. We had no guarantee that the securities would be there. And, most important, whether the evidence was found there or not, once the warrant was served I would be heated up. My cover would be blown. Against Lyle's objections, I also decided not to wear a wire during the meeting. I knew from Cliff's savvy about wires that he might have me checked, and I didn't want to take that chance.

"What about the hundred K?" I asked. "We don't have much time to come up with it."

"I'll phone Jim King, but the local SAC office won't have that much buy money. We'll have to get it from the ivory tower."

I kept a low profile for the next two days, except for taking a couple of Ritmo's pestering calls. He did his part to keep the deal alive and secure his sliver of the pie. On Thursday afternoon, I met Lyle at a roadside country store we had used as a meeting place several times before. He got into the seat next to me in the Camaro. The stitches were gone from his chin and the thin cut line had turned pink. He handed me a medium-sized brown paper bag. I opened the bag and he said, "A cool hundred grand. Clean bills. Special ops hot-shot them from Washington." He then handed me a standard government cash receipt form, which I signed.

"You think Cliff will sign one of these for me?" I joked.

We again discussed the wire, and Lyle pushed hard this time. "I want you wired, Tony. I want to hear what's going on in there in case we have to kick the door in."

"Relax, big boy. Cliff buys the act."

"Yeah, but a lot of other things can go wrong."

"No dice. Just tell me about the other security arrangements."

"Our man at the bar will be wearing a blue t-shirt and a Yankee baseball cap. A man-woman team will be seated as a couple in a nearby booth. The female agent is blonde in a white top. She's got big headlights so you won't miss her."

I arrived at The Gallop around eleven o'clock that night. I spotted Lyle and a partner circling around the club in his G-car and knew there was an additional surveillance team in the area. Inside, Ritmo paced back and forth behind the bar. I carried a small briefcase containing the buy money, and set it down next to me. There were a few regulars at the bar, as well as the undercover agent in the Yankee cap. Several tables were filled with patrons from the track. The ATF couple was in position, seated in a booth. The agents blended in well with the regulars.

Ritmo kept looking around the club and was not his usually cool self. He didn't pour me the customary drink. "Cliff's here, it's all set," he told me. He looked toward the front door several times and asked, "Anybody with you?"

"Should there be, Ritmo? Are you worried about me, or Cliff?"

"I just figured you might have some backup, but you won't need it. Everything's cool." He then reached under the bar and pushed the button that signaled into the office. A minute later, Cliff Dubroc appeared in the doorway. He stared for a moment, and surveyed the club in his usual manner, standing behind his professor-like, wire-rimmed glasses. He looked at Ritmo, then me, and nodded toward the office door.

I took a deep breath, grabbed the briefcase, and walked into the office. Ritmo closed the door behind me and didn't enter the room. I had gone over the deal many times in my head and planned to make the transaction brief. But I wasn't ready for the first thing I saw when I walked in. Seated in a corner chair behind Cliff's desk was Phil Tanzini, *the Ice Pick*. He was neatly groomed, as always, and wore an expensive suit over an open-collared silk shirt. His legs were crossed, and he sat back in the chair in a relaxed manner. My heart rate shot up at this surprise. I tried to keep my breathing normal. I went directly on the offensive.

"What the fuck is this?"

Cliff answered softly, "Relax, Tony. We're all friends here." Tanzini said nothing. "Keep your piece if it makes you feel good, but we're gonna check you for a wire."

Tanzini got up and told me to kneel on the seat of a chair, facing him. I removed my coat and took the .38 from my waistband. I spread my arms out, and held the gun in my right hand. The muzzle was only inches from Tanzini's head but didn't seem to bother him at all. He unbuttoned my shirt, then had me drop my pants and shorts around my knees. What a picture this made. Tanzini was a pro, and had checked for wires before. Satisfied, he stepped back and said, "He's clean."

I barked angrily at both of them. "Are you guys finished looking at my nuts?"

"Okay, Tony," Cliff answered. "Don't be insulted, it's business."

"The business is between us. What's this guy doing here?" I asked while I put my clothes back in place. I stuck the .38 back in the front of my waistband.

"He's my responsibility. Let's get on with it."

I let the remark slide, but all three of us knew it was the other way around – Cliff was the Ice Pick's responsibility. Law enforcement agencies knew Cliff Dubroc and The Gallop were connected, but until now nobody knew how. Some agencies even thought the connection was rumor and not fact, since Cliff's mafia partners were so well hidden. Tanzini was Luke Trombatore's protégé', and it was now clear that their visits to the area were not coincidental.

"The cash is here, all of it," I told Cliff. Five K stacks. Random Federal Reserve letters. Can't be traced. Count it if you want."

Tanzini stepped to the desk, clicked open the briefcase, then counted each of the thousand one-hundred dollar bills. He nodded, then shut the case and sat back down in his chair. Cliff opened the middle desk drawer and retrieved a sheath containing notes from the Commerce Bank and Trust Company of Louisiana. He handed it to me and I inspected the bundle. There were thirty notes in ten-thousand dollar denominations, and ten notes in twenty-thousand dollar denominations - a half-million dollars in negotiable securities.

The whole time I checked the notes, I kept an eye on Tanzini. I knew his reputation with the ice pick and that he could kill me swiftly and silently in a matter of seconds. If he did, they would have the cash and still keep the notes. I hoped they knew how hot the notes were and didn't want to keep them anyway. Tanzini went to a small cabinet and turned his back to me. My eyes darted between him and Cliff. I wrapped my fingers around the butt of my .38 as he turned back around facing me with something in his hand. I relaxed when I saw it was a bottle of amaretto. He placed three shot glasses on the desk and filled them with the almond liqueur. He handed one to me and raised a toast with one of the few words he spoke the entire time, "*Saluta!*"

We downed the shots, then I buttoned my coat and headed to the door. I turned to Tanzini and said, "My regards to Luke." He raised another shot, threw back his head, and slammed it down. I winked at Ritmo on the way out. He grinned so broadly at my gesture that he exposed a gold tooth on the side of his face I hadn't seen before. I unbuttoned my coat, which signaled the undercover agents in the club that I was okay. The absence of my briefcase also let them know that the buy had gone down.

Back in my car, I flashed the headlights to give Lyle and the surveillance teams the same message. Lyle followed me in a circuitous route to the parking lot of the Lafayette Hilton. We got out of our cars and I couldn't hold back a smile as I threw the bank notes on the hood of his G-car. I dated and initialed each note in the bottom right-hand corner. Lyle did the same, then placed them in a large manila envelope with ATF EVIDENCE stamped in bold print across the front. He sealed the envelope, and we both signed and dated it.

"Two cats in the bag," he said.

"Three cats. Phil Tanzini was there, checked me for a wire." Lyle's face dropped, and he spoke quietly.

"Jesus Christ. If you wired up like I wanted, we'd be cutting an ice pick out of your belly right now."

"Forget it, Lyle. Cliff and the local thugs might kill an agent, but the guys on Tanzini's level wouldn't."

"Maybe not. But they *would* kill an informer, and they had no way to know if you're an agent or a snitch."

"Bullshit. I would have sung loud and clear, like a tenor in *La Traviata*."

Lyle laughed. "I can picture that. Hey, I have to roll. Those assholes are holding a hundred grand of Uncle Sam's money. We'll need more agents to keep an eye on the cash. Poker keeps going up." Lyle threw his car into gear and headed to meet the surveillance teams.

We now knew that Cliff, Ritmo, and the club were mobbed up through Phil Tanzini and Luke Trombatore. The connection was what probably made Ritmo's pardon for his murder conviction possible. The Gallop was Trombatore's club, or at least it operated under his control. We had Tanzini directly involved with the bank notes, but Trombatore had insulated himself from the buy. He was also insulated from the club as far as any documentation was concerned. Besides the securities case itself, we had put together the pieces of the puzzle for The Gallop.

I stayed away from the club for the next several days to let the deal digest and to stay out of Cliff's face. I followed the local news about Ronald Reagan's campaign visit, and watched part of his speech on television from my room. A pan shot of the candidate's speech got my attention. Next to the speaker's podium was the familiar, blue-black, mop-top haircut of Ernie Chinn. He assumed the usual stance with his back straight, hands held together in front of him. A coiled earplug wire ran down his neck. He occasionally lifted his left wrist to his mouth and spoke a few words into the mike hidden under the cuff of his sleeve. His head slowly turned back and forth and he reminded me of a Chinese bobble-head doll. I watched the rest of the speech, mainly to see Ernie and any other agents I might recognize on the detail. I decided to have some fun and phoned Lyle.

"Any of our guys on the Reagan detail?"

"Of course. Why?"

"Is the detail staying overnight or moving on?"

"I don't know, and if I did I couldn't tell you."

"Yeah, sure. Find out and let me know where they crash for the night, okay?"

Fifteen minutes later, Lyle called back and gave me the name of the hotel. I waited until about three hours after the speech and called there.

"Connect me with Mr. Ernie Chinn."

A sleepy voice answered. I imagined him jumping up from his sleep to answer the phone, a common occurrence for him.

"What is it?"

"Wake up you slanty-eyed motherfucker." I used the best Cajun accent I could muster. There was silence on the other end, then the sound of rustling on the night table. I knew he was scurrying around for a pen and note pad. When he was ready, he answered.

"Who's this?"

"One who knows. Go back to what you're good at, cleaning laundry."

He seethed through the phone. But he was a professional, and a potential problem for the detail from a crazy caller was more important to him than personal insult. He was fully awake by now and started asking lots of questions. I answered each one with a silly answer in my fake Cajun voice. Finally, I gave him a big clue and let him off the hook.

"Have you been surfing lately?"

"Well, if it ain't Mussolini himself. How the hell did you find me tucked in here? My wife can't even locate me."

"My secret. Are you okay?"

"Sure, what about you? I thought you were some *nutso* I'd have to write a report about. Are you back in the world yet?"

"Not yet. I'll be in touch when I am. Hey, I thought you were sipping martinis with Rockefeller."

"I am, but this is Reagan's swan song and they wanted to rotate a few fresh faces around him. I'll be back with Rocky after the convention. By the way, you lucky bastard, if you drag out your case a few more weeks you'll miss the convention.

"Yeah, ain't that a shame."

"When I see you I want to know how you found me on a one-day whistle stop."

"No chance. But I'll leave you with this. . . If you're still in Lafayette for lunch tomorrow, take Reagan to Prejean's and order the seafood platter."

"Huh?"

"*Ciao, Ernie.*" I hung up and enjoyed a laugh. The next morning, the papers and news reports made no mention of major robberies or burglaries during the candidate's visit. Ritmo had taken my advice.

CHAPTER 22

Race 5...

Six Furlongs. Purse $15,000. For three and four year old maidens. Claiming Price $20,000.

The conditions of the fifth race on the program signaled an uneventful contest limited to horses that had never won a race. Most of the nags weren't worth a fraction of the claiming price, and twenty thousand dollars probably could have bought all ten horses in the race. But horses have a better chance to get their first win against other maidens, then usually start at the top of the claiming ranks and work their way down in value. T-Red was running a four year old maiden for one of his trainers and invited me to come along.

"I don't have a racing commission license, Red. I can't get into the paddock or the backstretch barn area."

"You don't need one. The horse's owner lives in Houston and he never comes to watch this cockroach run. Dress like an owner and act like one. Nobody will notice you don't have an ID badge. Those who do won't care."

We stood in the open paddock stall and waited for the jockeys to make their short walk from the jock's room to the saddling area. T-Red stood directly in front of the colt named Richter Scale and jiggled the reins near the horse's mouth to keep him distracted. He was an average looking, penny-red chestnut with a wide white blaze that ran from just below his ears to his muzzle. Like most thoroughbreds he was high-strung, and although this was his seventh career start, he was jittery and kept lifting his feet in place. The stall was cramped, so I was careful to stand far enough away from him that he couldn't stomp his nine hundred pounds down on my foot.

"He's not a true greenie, Red, so why so nervous?"

"This is his first time running under the lights, he don't know what to make of it."

A short, squat man of about sixty in a worn brown suit and oversized tie walked up and down in front of the paddock holding a clipboard. He visited each stall, and when he got to ours he walked up to the colt and studied the white markings on his coat. He flipped up the horse's upper lip, exposing a numbered tattoo. He compared it to the number on Richter Scale's foal papers that were clamped to his clipboard, to be sure they matched.

"What's the matter, you old bastard?" T-Red asked, "think we're gonna run a ringer on you?"

"Nope," the man replied without looking up, "not you Red, you're too fucking stupid to pull off something like that." The rumpled racing official then took the few steps to stall number eight to officially identify the next horse. Pierre D'Argonne, Richter Scale's trainer, joined us in the stall. He was a heavyset Cajun in his mid-fifties, and wore a tan Stetson hat and a disinterested look. A khaki-clad jockey's valet strode in behind him carrying the horse's racing tack. He threw a white saddlecloth with a large, black number seven stitched on it up onto the horse's withers. On top of that he threw a small leather saddle, then held it in place as the trainer tightened the elastic girth and buckled it under the horse's torso. The valet, easily identified as an ex-jockey from his height and build, double-checked the security of the saddle with a forceful tug. He said nothing during the process, and only gave a hushed "Good luck" as he walked back to the jockey's room to prep tack for the next race.

D'Argonne, who barely glanced at me as T-Red introduced us, said a few words in French. Then T-Red reached into the back pocket of his jeans and pulled out a thin strip of white cloth about two feet long and handed it to the trainer. T-Red remained facing the horse directly in front of him, holding the reins near the bit while D'Argonne reached into the colt's mouth and grabbed the end of his long, rubbery tongue with one hand. With the other, he wrapped the tongue tie several times around the middle of the tongue, then drew the ends down under the muzzle and tied them together in a neat bow. He let go, and now the tongue was tied in place; it couldn't slip over the bit or slip back to block the horse's air passage during the exertion of the race. T-Red then retrieved a small cobalt-blue jar from his hip pocket. D'Argonne dug his index and middle fingers into the Vick's VapoRub and smeared the glob a few inches up each of Richter Scale's nostrils. The stall filled with a potent menthol smell from the horse's first exhale. Then, as if for good measure, the trainer opened the horse's mouth again and wiped the remaining jelly on his tied tongue. D'Argonne was an assembly line trainer, but used the time-tested methods that opened the air passages and allowed the horse to draw in the maximum amount of oxygen during his race. Almost no words were exchanged during the whole process, which T-Red and D'Argonne had obviously gone through together many times before.

    T-Red stepped to the side of the colt and led him to join the line of horses in the walking ring. They walked the oblong path that allowed the fans pressed against the grandstand fence, and those watching from above behind the glass walls of the clubhouse, to view the entries. They could get a close-up view to help select which horse they wanted to back with their wagers. Some would eliminate betting on any horse with racing bandages, or those running with extra equipment like blinkers or shadow rolls. The less sophisticated handicappers would undoubtedly base their picks on inconsequential things like the horse's color, or how many involuntary craps he took in the walking ring.

    D'Argonne and I remained in the stall for only a minute when the jockey appeared. He was a journeyman rider. He gave the trainer a customary handshake, then turned to me and did the same. He tapped some mud from his shiny patent leather boots with his whip and asked D'Argonne, "What's my instructions, boss?"

    "Go the front, then improve your position."

    The jock laughed and replied with a short, "Okay."

    The grooms led the horses back to their respective stalls, and the horse identifier in the brown suit, clipboard still in hand, went to the middle of the paddock area and shouted, "Rider's up!" D'Argonne grabbed the bottom of the jockey's boot and legged him up onto the colt's back. T-Red walked the chestnut, whose color was now darker from nervous sweat, and his rider in numerical order with the other horses to the opening in the rail and onto the track surface. He joined D'Argonne and me, and as we entered the grandstand area the trainer muttered something in French and walked away.

"What'd he say, Red?"

"He said this horse will run like he's in quicksand. Don't bet a nickel on him."

I heeded the advice, and noticed that neither T-Red nor D'Argonne made a trip to the betting windows. The race started cleanly, and true to his past performances, Richter Scale broke in the middle of the pack and stayed there for most of the race. In the turn for home, something interesting happened. Several of the front runners ran out of gas, a common occurrence in maiden races, and Richter Scale emerged from his mediocre position to finish a distant second behind a strong betting favorite. His run down the stretch created the general illusion that happens in most races. It looked as if he was gaining velocity down the stretch, when in reality he was passing tired horses. He had more left than they did when it counted, and he paid seven dollars to place for a two-dollar ticket. We were slightly surprised at the colt's second place finish, but also aware that maiden races are the most unpredictable.

The veteran jockey jogged Richter Scale back to the finish line where we met him on the track. The faces of the horse and jockey were both splattered with small clumps of sand thrown back at them by the front runners during most of the race. The jockey flipped his dirt-covered goggles up onto his helmet, which exposed a clean area of skin around his eyes. The rest of his face was masked in sand, as was the face, neck, and chest of Richter Scale. He dismounted with a bounce, unbuckled the saddle, and cradled it under one arm. T-Red grabbed the horse's reins and D'Argonne waited for the jock to finish the post race weigh-in to assure that the horse carried his exact assigned weight for the duration of the race.

A racing official clamped a black plastic disk with a large, white number two stamped on it onto the colt's bit, identifying him as the second place finisher. He shouted to no one in particular, "Richter Scale to the spit box." I walked alongside T-Red, who led the horse across the track to the infield. D'Argonne and the jockey walked side-by-side down Alibi Alley, the rail area leading back to the paddock, where jockeys have a minute during that walk to explain to the horse's trainer what happened during the race. After every race, on every track, there is only one jockey - the winner - who doesn't have to come up with an alibi. The others have an ample supply of excuses for why they didn't win. The race was too long for the horse. The race was too short. The horse needs blinkers. He needs an outside post position. He got hemmed in. He needed this race. The list is endless, and includes stories of bad racing luck, but never includes the possibility that the horse got a bad ride from the jockey. Every conversation in Alibi Alley ends more or less the same way, when the rider tells the trainer, "Put me back on him, boss, and next time we'll get the gravy."

Richter Scale's excitement from the race overtook his exhaustion, and he pranced as we walked across the infield path to the backstretch. We passed horses and their handlers going in the opposite direction, toward the paddock, to saddle up for the next race. "Look at him," T-Red cracked as we hurried our step to keep up with the horse, "he thinks he's done something because he didn't finish in back of the pack again." His disdainful words couldn't conceal his pride, and he patted the colt on the neck. "He might turn out to be a racehorse after all."

As we tromped across the infield in the sandy soil, several white egrets with pointed yellow beaks, inhabitants of the swamp adjacent to the track, stood motionless in the tall grass alongside us. I chuckled, pointed them out to T-Red and said, "They remind me of the pink flamingoes in the infield at Gulfstream Park in Miami."

"Yeah," he answered, "they're the Coon-ass version."

We walked past several barns and reached the test barn of the Louisiana Racing Commission. I sat on a long wooden bench with several owners and trainers of the first and second place finishers in previous races. T-Red checked his horse in with a small, wiry man who examined and recorded the tattoo number under his lip. Several commission employees watched impassively as T-Red walked his charge in circles behind other grooms and horses cooling out, stopping occasionally to draw water from buckets specifically designated for each horse. The wiry man watched the race results on a television in the small office and prepared paperwork for the next pair sent for drug testing. I recalled the old days when the spit box was called so because swabs of saliva were taken as test samples.

After thirty minutes, the man emerged from the office and grabbed a long aluminum pole with a thick plastic bag attached to the end. "Okay, let's try," he shouted to T-Red, who was making a circle at the far end of the barn. He pointed to a stall with thick straw bedding, where T-Red deposited his horse. The man ordered T-Red out of the stall, and he entered and stood in a corner. He began a series of whistles, one high followed by one low, the method used to get horses to urinate. Within a minute, the colt positioned himself in the middle of the stall, stretched out all four legs, and began to pee. The man reached his metal pole under the horse, and collected at least a pint of the yellow liquid. He sealed the bag and filled out tags identifying the sample. He instructed T-Red to sign the labels along with him. He then walked over to a machine and lowered the sample into a frozen liquid for only a few seconds. When he lifted the sample bag back up, it was frozen solid.

"I make piss-sicles for a living," he said without expression. He placed the frozen bag into a freezer, to be sent to the testing laboratory at Louisiana State University. The LSU lab would screen for a myriad of drugs that can enhance a horse's performance. A positive test would uphold the purse money to the horse's owner and also subject the trainer, ultimately responsible for anything to do with the horse, to suspension or revocation of his racing license.

T-Red took Richter Scale back to his home barn, and I returned to the grandstand to watch the remaining races. I was impressed with the security and chain of custody measures used by the racing commission for detecting illegal drugs in the horses. Under their procedures it would be difficult, if not impossible, to affect the outcome of a race by hopping a horse with drugs without being detected. The test barn employees were nonchalant but competent, and the system was tough to beat. Or so I thought.

CHAPTER 23

The guard shack at the entrance to the backstretch of Evangeline Downs was a small metal building painted dull orange. I pulled up to the gate and a uniformed guard stuck his head out of the shack and asked, "What you want *mon ami*?"

"I'm looking for T-Red LeBlanc."

The guard looked me over, then with the laid-back attitude I had gotten used to in this part of the country, he said, "Check in the track kitchen, on your left." He didn't ask my name, or for any identification, nor did he record my license plate number. He leaned over a counter and pushed a button, and a small electric motor pulled back the gate to a chain link fence blocking the entrance. He waved me through the gate.

I drove slowly down the narrow road that ran between a long row of tin-roofed stables. I stopped often for horses that crossed the road. They were led to or from the race track by exercise boys and grooms. I pulled up in front of a large building on the left. It was a converted stable with a big sign that read *Kitchen* hung over the double door entrance.

This was the unofficial nerve center of the race track. The room was large, with high ceilings. There were chunks of dry sand and tobacco spatterings all over the floor, brought in by the backstretch personnel. The room was filled with workers who sat or stood around dozens of tables. Some were young jockeys and exercise riders, their heads crowned with riding helmets. Some were horse owners, trainers, grooms, and the hot-walkers who cooled out the horses after the morning workouts. Jockey agents huddled together with their appointment books, and studied the list of horses entering races that day. They hustled the trainers to give mounts to their respective riders. Feed and hay merchants, tack salesmen, blacksmiths, and veterinarians all mingled together. Most of their chatter was in Cajun French. They came and went. None lingered for long, as they hurried to get the morning's work done before the track closed for training at ten o'clock.

I sat at an empty table, enjoyed a hot cup of coffee, and waited for T-Red to show up. Occasionally one of the men, or one of the few women in the room, walked by me with the smell of horse manure on their boots. From behind I felt a hand on my shoulder, then a small figure walked around me and sat at my table. It was old Comeaux. His gray hair was disheveled and his work clothes were soaked with perspiration. The mixture of sweat and dirt gave his worn denim shirt the texture of canvas. He wore rubber boots that were caked in mud and straw.

"You're working too hard, Comeaux. Where's your help?"

"A poor Coon-ass like me can't afford help . . . not and feed the horses, too."

"Coffee's on me, old timer."

"*Merci.*"

We talked about the horses, and I told him that I was looking for T-Red. After a few minutes, he downed what was left of the thick, black Cajun coffee, and got up to leave.

"He's in stable seven. I'll tell him you're here if I see him."

I read the Daily Racing Form and waited. I was interrupted by a shout from the tall, heavyset woman standing behind the cash register. She yelled at me from across the room and pointed to a food tray T-Red was holding. He stood in front of her and grinned. I walked over and paid for his breakfast. Before she could count out my change, T-Red signaled to a man working behind a bar next to the cafeteria line. The man reached into a cooler and lobbed a can at T-Red, which he snatched and set down on the tray. I frowned, and told the cashier to add the can to the check. We walked back to my spot and T-Red emptied the contents of his tray onto the table – bacon, eggs, toast - and beer.

"You're a cheap bastard, Red."

"Hey. . . if you didn't want something you wouldn't be here, so ante up."

"I need one last thing from you."

"You guys never have a *last* thing. What is it?" T-Red shoveled the food into his mouth between gulps of beer. I leaned over the table and told him that I needed a cool place to meet Frank Duplessis outside of St. Landry Parish.

"Why?"

"He's well-heeled in his home parish, and we might not get him prosecuted there, especially because of the corruption."

"But you guys are fucking feds. You don't need the locals to prosecute."

"All we have on him right now is murder conspiracy. That's a state charge no matter who makes the case. I need to close the deal with him in Acadia Parish, where we're more likely to get the case prosecuted. Any ideas?"

He scratched his stubbled face and answered slowly. "There's an old bar on Highway Thirteen near Rayne, called the Blue Goose. It's a rough-and-tumble joint that doesn't do much business, only local trade. Frank knows the place, you can get him there."

I took out a fifty-dollar bill and handed it to T-Red. The payment didn't look out of place since most of the backstretch workers were paid in cash. "I'm waiting here for another thirty minutes. If Frank doesn't come in, I want you to give him the message that I'm back in town. Tell him to call me at The Plantation."

Later that afternoon Frank Duplessis called. His voice was calm over the phone, even calculated. "Been looking for you. I've got that stuff you wanted, all of it. Where and when? We need to meet soon."

"Tomorrow night at ten. Parking lot of the Blue Goose in Rayne."

"Why there?"

"Away from town, from so many eyes and ears."

He hesitated for a moment, as if the location made him suspicious. Then he answered, "I'll be there."

The following night I met Lyle and Special Agent Jerry Lofton for dinner at the Lafayette Hilton. Lofton was one of ATF's technical experts from the dirty tricks squad, highly trained in electronic surveillance. He was a tall, mild mannered, bookish man who asked few questions about the case. I gave them the layout of the meeting to take place with Frank Duplessis. Lyle already had cased the Blue Goose. He explained that there would be a team of agents dressed in hunting gear inside the bar, as well as another surveillance team placed in a car a couple of miles away. Lyle told Lofton he needed to wire me with a transmitter instead of a recorder. He and Lofton would record the transmission in their G-car a mile away from the meeting.

"Get your gadgets together and we'll meet in your room at eight-thirty," Lyle told Lofton. The agent quietly got up from the table and left.

"I hate wires, Lyle. But without this one, we don't have much evidence, only my word against Frank's. I hope he's not too hip about checking me."

We finished going over the game plan for the meeting. Before we left to join Lofton, Lyle leaned over the table and gave me a serious look. "I want to remind you of something, Tony."

"What is it?"

"I know I screwed up pushing for a wire on the Cliff Dubroc deal. But even though you didn't know Tanzini would be involved, you were ready for them. You knew you were dealing with hardened criminals. You knew how they act and what they might try. With this Duplessis guy, you've got a question mark. You don't know who he wants killed, or why. From what we gathered on him we know he's a mean prick. Expect the unexpected."

"Thanks for the warning, but I'm ahead of you. I'd rather deal with ten Tanzini's than one of these off-the-wall guys."

We met Lofton in his hotel room. He had several black, plastic attaché' cases spread on the bed and on the small table in the room. Some were open, which exposed intricate needle gauges and knob controls. Small red and yellow lights beamed from inside the cases; some of them blinked. Lofton took a thin, gold-colored wire from a cellophane package, and told me to remove my shirt. He stretched the wire from the small of my back, around my side, and up the front of my stomach to mid-chest. He slowly and carefully taped the entire length of wire to my skin with a special skin-colored adhesive tape. The only part of the wire now exposed was the last inch on each end. I looked in the large mirror on the wall, and the long tape reminded me of a surgical scar.

"Turn around, Tony," Lofton instructed.

I turned my back toward him, and through the mirror I watched him place a small battery pack that looked like a credit card into the small of my back. He applied the tape over it, and plugged the wire into the pack. Lyle sat on the edge of the bed, and watched the procedure like a boy sitting on a curb watching a construction site.

Lofton then held a tiny, cylinder-shaped microphone, no bigger than a grain of rice, which he plugged into the end of the wire on my chest. He used several testing devices to check the transmitter and spent a few minutes adjusting the controls in one of the attaché' cases. He tapped his finger onto the end of the mike and a loud, thumping sound came from the case. He double checked the strength of the battery pack and said, "All set."

I buttoned up my shirt as Lofton removed his gun from a dresser drawer and shoved it into his shoulder holster. "How does it feel?" he asked.

I twisted my body back and forth and felt the tape pull at my skin. "Stiff," I answered. My voice came out of a speaker in the case that rested on the table.

"Good, that means the tape is holding." Lofton looked at both of us. "Okay guys, you've got two hours, tops, out of the battery pack. After that the mike goes dead. Get your business done as quickly as possible."

Before we left the room I felt a moderate stinging-burning sensation from the wire. I had worn them before, but had forgotten how uncomfortable they were. Lofton explained that the wire would not get any hotter. But if it cooled off altogether, it meant the battery was dead and it would no longer transmit. Lyle helped Lofton carry his equipment to their car, and I got on with the business of forgetting about the wire.

I took the Camaro west out of Lafayette to Rayne, Louisiana and drove to the Blue Goose. Lyle and Lofton, as well as the other vehicle surveillance team, lagged a couple of miles behind, far out of sight. During the thirty minute drive I sang along with the radio, recited dumb poems, blew raspberries, and whistled, just to aggravate Lyle and Lofton, who were forced to listen to every sound. They could hear me but had no way to respond. I laughed out loud at the thought.

The bar was an old wooden-framed building located on an isolated section of two-lane highway. It resembled a hunting camp. A large, screened porch wrapped around the front and sides. The shelled parking lot and the building itself were dimly lit. An old, rusted, Dixie Beer sign hung from a metal pole out front with Blue Goose painted across the top of the sign.

I spoke to Lyle through the mike and gave him my position in the parking lot. I fought the natural tendency to bend my head toward the mike. "It's ten minutes after ten. There's a few pickup trucks in the lot, but not Frank's. I'm parked on the east side of the bar."

Twenty more minutes passed, and Frank Duplessis had not shown. Several thoughts came to mind, and I shared them with Lyle through the wire. "After all this, Duplessis gets cold feet? Is this another bullshit case that doesn't materialize?" I knew the covering agents were as apprehensive as I was, but the veterans had been through this kind of thing before. Just then, a set of high beam headlights appeared behind me. Duplessis had arrived, some forty minutes late. "The subject is here. Start your tape," I said into the mike.

Duplessis got out of his pickup and got into the passenger seat of my car. He placed a medium-sized flat cardboard box onto the console between us. The box rattled a little and made a thud when he put it down. "Ten grand," he muttered. "The other ten when it's done, right?"

"Fucking A," I told him.

"Everything you need for the job is in there."

I unfolded the top of the box and pulled out a stack of bills that totaled ten thousand dollars, neatly wrapped in a paper bank band. I placed the money back in the box and removed a vintage Colt .38 special caliber revolver. The gun had a four inch barrel that had been threaded an inch from the end. Next to the gun was a steel pipe that threaded onto the end of the gun. I screwed it onto the muzzle, then unscrewed it and put it back in the box.

"That's the silencer," Duplessis said. I haven't tried it myself, but it'll work."

I didn't answer and checked out the other items in the box: a folding pocket knife, a length of quarter-inch nylon rope, and a roll of gray duct tape.

"What's all this crap?" I asked.

Duplessis then threw me a curve ball. He said the man he wanted murdered lived in Crowley, a town several miles away. "Let's go, I'll show you his house." I had hoped to complete the immediate deal with him there in the parking lot, but I was forced to go with the flow. He directed me into Crowley, about fifteen minutes away, and during the ride explained his motive. "Antoine Broussard fucked up my life." I said little and hoped to get as much of his story transmitted to tape as possible.

"I threw my wife out a few months ago. She went to live with her elderly parents. Then she started dating Broussard. He's got money and lots of it. I'll never pry her away from that." Duplessis described in great detail his plan for how to kill Broussard. He directed me to an upscale residential area in downtown Crowley. He pointed out a large, two-story, antebellum style white frame residence with large columns in front. A wide, semi-circle driveway in the middle of the front yard led to the main entrance of the house.

"The primary elections are Saturday. Broussard is a poll commissioner, he'll be checking the voting precincts. They close at eight o'clock. About eight-thirty he'll pull his car into the carport on the west side of the big house and go inside through a side door. That's where you can jump him and force him inside."

"Who else lives here?"

"Just him, that rotten sonofabitch. But Danielle will be with him."

"Danielle?"

"My wife."

"Wait a minute..."

"Don't worry, I don't want you to kill her."

I parked the car around the corner from the house and turned to Duplessis. "You didn't tell me anything about somebody else being involved."

He looked directly at me. His eyes were opened wide, as if in a trance. He spoke excitedly. "I want you to tie her up. Bind her hands and feet. Then beat her. Make her suffer. Slap her face. Kick her in the tits. But don't kill her. And call her a whore. Loud! In her ear! Make him watch. Then blow his brains out in front of her. Cut off his dick and shove it in her mouth, then tape it shut. Leave her there tied up near the body until somebody finds her."

Now I knew why the other items were in his cardboard box along with the gun and silencer. His eyes had the strangest look I had ever seen. He seemed to get off on just telling me about it, like a man whose dream was finally coming true. I sat silent for a minute and hoped the wire was transmitting. It still burned my skin, which was a good indication.

"I'll have to kill her, Frank. She's a witness."

"No! No! No!" He shook his head side to side. "I want her back. But I want the bitch to pay for what she's done. And if she watches him die she'll know it's over. She'll have to come back to me."

I didn't want to overplay my hand, so I fanned the cash he paid me back at the Blue Goose. "Okay, you've got a deal."

On the drive back to the bar I checked the time and it was almost eleven-thirty. The battery pack was losing power by now, so I sped up and kept Duplessis talking. We arrived in the parking lot and I said, "Have my other ten grand here Saturday night. If your times are correct, I'll be here at nine-thirty."

"No. I want to hear on the news the following day about what happened. That way I know you did it and you're not ripping me off."

"Bullshit, Frank. I'm not sticking around here that long. I'll be hundreds of miles away by Sunday. You meet me here right after it's over and I'll bring you proof that he's dead."

"What proof?"

"I'll cut his tongue out and bring it to you. His ear, his eye, what do you want?" I was bluffing, but it worked. Duplessis recoiled at the idea.

He thought for a minute, then said, "Bring me his wallet, his papers, his wristwatch. I'll know he's dead."

"You'll get it. And be sure you're here with my fucking money or I'll hunt your ass down too."

Before he got out of the car, Duplessis turned back and said, "Be sure, Tony. Be sure to beat her in the face. And don't forget to call her a whore."

"Yeah, sure."

He got into his truck and drove away. I just sat for a couple of minutes and thought about the bizarre murder plot that had just unfolded. Duplessis had followed Broussard for some time and knew his activities and habits. He certainly wanted Broussard eliminated from competition. But in a strange way, the victim was no more than a prop in his plan to humiliate his wife and drive her back to him. I leaned back in the seat, let out a sigh, and spoke into the mike.

"You guys got that? What a sick bastard."

I carried the box of items Duplessis gave me up to agent Jerry Lofton's room at the Hilton. I couldn't wait to get the wire and adhesive tape off. When I arrived, Lofton was securing his equipment. Lyle was busy on the phone with the surveillance agents.

"Did you copy everything over the wire?" I asked.

Lofton grinned. "Clear as a bell, we heard every word."

I hurried to unbutton my shirt. Lofton stopped what he was doing and directed his attention to retrieving the gear from my body. He slowly unplugged the small mike, then the wire from the battery pack. He cut the adhesive tape parallel to the wire. He stopped suddenly and looked straight at me. "There's only two ways to do this, Tony. Which way do you want it?"

"Rip it off."

"Are you sure you don't want the slow peel?"

I braced myself and said, "Get on with it."

He walked around me and manipulated the tape that was stuck so tightly to the skin on my back. He dug his fingernails under the tape, then with both hands pulled sideways with a force that almost threw me into the mirror. I yelled with pain as the tape tore away. Lofton then spun me around and grabbed the end of the tape on my chest. With the same force, he pulled down with a sudden jerk. I was unable to muffle a scream as the tape pulled off a wide path of hair from my chest and stomach.

"Sorry, pal. But all that tape beats having the wire fall down your ass crack in the middle of a deal."

Through the mirror I saw a two-inch wide, red welt down the middle of my body. Lofton pointed to a bottle of rubbing alcohol and cotton balls on his dresser. I used it to remove the remainder of adhesive on my skin. When the pain subsided, Lyle and I sat at the table and examined the contents of the box from Duplessis.

The wad of money was wrapped in two white paper bank bands with $5,000 printed on each, along with the words "Lafayette Savings & Loan." The Colt .38 was a six-shot revolver that was originally blue steel, but was now a gray color from age and wear. "An oldie but a goodie," Lyle said.

There were six rounds of .38 special ammunition inside a small coin envelope, along with a six-inch blade pocketknife, a one-hundred foot length of nylon rope, and a roll of duct tape. Except for the bullets, all the items were new. The silencer was hand-machined, a double-cylinder length of pipe with steel wool packed inside and holes drilled through it to muffle sound. Lofton finished packing his gadgets and joined us at the table. We passed the items around to each other for closer examination. I peered at the evidence and said, "A sick bastard, but what an amateur. Silencers don't work on revolvers. The sound and blast comes out of the cylinder even if the muzzle is muffled. And look at this other shit. He probably went to the corner hardware store and bought it."

"Doesn't something bother you about that?" Lyle asked. "This guy is committed. He made sure you got everything you need to carry out his execution in detail. It's scary to know there are sickos like this out there."

"Every gun has at least one story behind it," Lofton said as he looked at the Colt. "This gun was made before World War Two, when few records were kept. We probably can't trace it. Even though the silencer generally won't quiet a revolver, if it muffles a minimum number of decibels we've got him on possession of an assassination device."

"You're right," Lyle added. "We'll wait for the lab tests on that one. But we knew going in that we might not get the federal case. So what? We've got his ass nailed on the murder contract, and we got him in Acadia Parish. He can't get the charges deep-sixed there. When he shows up Saturday with the other half of the money, we slam the door on him."

"This doesn't concern me, guys," Lofton said, "but how are you going to convince Duplessis that Broussard is dead?"

I looked at Lyle. "We can pull it off. Get the scoop on Broussard and Danielle Duplessis." I looked at the items in the box, then back up at the other men. "We don't need a wire Saturday. The risk of Duplessis searching me is greater than the need for more tapes on him. We've got plenty already. So . . . no wire. You can take your clandestine doodads back to Washington, Jerry." They nodded in agreement.

"Then I guess I'm done here," Lofton said. "I'll send you a copy of tonight's tapes as soon as I get the originals processed. Good luck, boys."

Assassin Hunter

CHAPTER 24

"Stake me to a couple of C-notes," T-Red spoke softly out of the side of his mouth.

"Sure," I answered, "but if you win I get the stake back. Fat chance, since you haven't won since Columbus came over."

I rapped on the entrance to the tack shop, a rusted metal door with remnants of gray paint that was full of small dents. The old wooden building with tin roofing sat back from the shell road just outside track property. It was a Tuesday night, which meant the track was dark. The weekly poker game provided relief to some of the gamblers who had withdrawal symptoms from not being able to bet the horses for a night. A dozen or so street characters floated in and out of the game, as well as race-trackers, depending on whose wallet was strong or weak. There was no telling who would be there on this night.

An apprentice jockey no more than sixteen years old answered the door and walked us through the shelves of horse liniment, vitamins, and salve concoctions. One-hundred pound sacks of oats lined the walls, and the store had a strong medicinal smell. We entered the smaller back room where four men and a woman sat around a large, round card table playing gin rummy to pass the time until more poker players arrived. I knew all of them. They cut the rummy game short when we arrived, and Pierre D'Argonne pointed for us to sit at the two empty chairs. His tan Stetson was cocked back on his head and he puffed thick smoke from the stub of a cheap cigar that contained more paper than tobacco. Phil Tanzini was seated directly across the table from me and winked at me silently as I sat down.

"Don't sit next to me, you fucking *Jonah*." A loud voice directed the words at T-Red and came from Cabbage Boy, a small black man in a sleeveless shirt that exposed well-developed shoulders and arms.

"Go play with yourself," T-Red shouted back while he unfolded the two hundred I had given him.

"Let's be gentlemen and play poker," D'Argonne interrupted.

"I don't want that hard luck bastard next to me," Cabbage Boy insisted. His face was drawn and had a large black cross tattooed on his cheekbones. I recognized it as the initiation cross, given to new juvenile inmates at the Louisiana correctional facility at Scotlandville. Since he was now about thirty years old, he had obviously carried this marker for a number of years. He had other prison tattoos on his arms, the crude permanent marks made by other inmates with India ink and safety pin needles. They verified that he was a convicted felon, having served time, and as such couldn't be licensed on most tracks. But he was only one of many granted licenses by the Louisiana racing commission for various reasons, one of which was the easy accessibility of governor's pardons. He was a freelance groom and hot-walker, and had brought stolen property to the game on a regular basis in order to convert it to quick cash.

"Sit here," I told T-Red. I got up out of my seat and took the one next to Cabbage Boy.

"A real diplomat," said Penny. He was a tall, bronze-skinned man who was always quick with a lighthearted comment. He was also a degenerate gambler who would rather gamble than eat. And he ate a lot. He had a large belly that hung over his beltless pants and wore old deck shoes with no socks. Rounding out the players was Dottie Sinclair, a tough thirty-five year old pony girl. Her stringy, straw colored hair fell around a sun-dried face that contained thousands of small reddish-brown freckles. She rode the lead horses, or ponies, that escorted the racehorses to the starting gate, and doubled as a groom for D'Argonne's assembly line in the mornings.

I usually gathered a lot of useless intelligence every week at this game. Besides the constant bickering and knocking each other, the conversation consisted of tall tales about the week's "sure thing" where a bundle would be bet on a horse that couldn't lose. Tonight's swag menu included fake Rolex watches, a couple of twenty-seven inch color TV sets still in shipping boxes, and an antique cameo ring probably stolen in a house burglary or purse snatching. The smaller stuff was passed around like a dessert cart for anyone interested, and the usual round of haggling over price triggered more arguments. The swag was mostly minor league, and none of it seemed important enough evidence for me to spend the government's money to buy it.

The game finally got underway, and four hours later T-Red was tapped out. Dottie, having lost her stake and borrowing another two hundred from D'Argonne, followed close behind. With only five players remaining, D'Argonne quit. Tanzini and I remained with Cabbage Boy and Penny, who had won about three hundred dollars, a week's pay for him. "How about a showdown hand for the three croakers?" he asked to any takers.

"You're on," Tanzini said, and they both stacked the money on the table. I shuffled the deck and had Penny cut the cards. I tossed five cards in rapid succession to each of them face up. Tanzini showed the highest hand with a mere Ace-Queen, but Penny's highest card was a Jack with none matching. Tanzini scooped up the money, and Penny shrugged his shoulders. He had played for hours to get three hundred up, then blew it all on a fifteen second card flip that required no skill. When everyone got up to leave, Tanzini grabbed me by the arm and said, "*Aspetta, paisano.*" I waited.

The teenager, who waited on the players and locked up the store, began cleaning up the empty beer bottles and ashtrays. Tanzini pulled a fifty-dollar bill from his roll and coiled his index finger at the boy. He folded the bill and dropped it into the kid's shirt pocket and said, "Give us a few minutes." The aspiring jockey bounced out of the back room and closed the door behind him. Tanzini and I remained, and Cabbage Boy hadn't moved from his chair beside me. "We've got a score working you might want in on," Tanzini said. Cabbage Boy leaned back in his chair and said nothing. I looked at Tanzini, and raised an eyebrow towards Cabbage Boy to ask if he should hear this. The Ice Pick nodded. "He's in. We need another guy with some *coglioni* to pull off a score. Listen to the plan. If you don't like the deal, just keep your mouth shut."

My brain went into overdrive with the possibilities. Did this involve the Duplessis murder contract? Why would Tanzini involve somebody like Cabbage Boy? The only thing I was certain of was that Luke Trombatore was involved. We had Tanzini on the securities buy, but needed something more to wrap up Trombatore.

"I'm listening."

"We're putting together a race for the boys in New Orleans. Tomorrow night."

"The only way I know to fix a race is to have all the jockeys in on it. Impossible. Getting ten pinheads to play along and keep their mouths shut is fool's play."

"Shut up and listen," he snapped. "The little burglars riding the horses won't know shit. We're gonna fix this race with hop." He stopped to get my reaction.

"It won't work. I've been to the spit box. They'll catch anything you use on a horse in the urine sample. It'll come right back to the horse's connections - owner, trainer, groom - with lots of digging around. No shot. Besides, some horses that are hit with stuff to make them hyper don't run any faster."

"You're a smart *Dago*," Tanzini said. But we're not gonna use hop on the winner. We're gonna drug the losers."

"What?"

"How many horses get sent to the spit box?" he asked.

"Two. The winner and second place finishers."

"Right. Now what happens if we don't try to speed up our horse, but we can slow down the rest of the field?"

It clicked. His scheme was to drug the other horses to make them run slower, and one particular horse, which wasn't drugged, would win and go to the test barn clean. "How in hell are you going to drug the entire field except for one horse?

"We don't have to," he smiled. "We've been waiting for a race like this, a perfect setup. It's for three thousand dollar claimers, the cheapest of the cheap horses. They're only a step away from the glue factory. Half the field is cripple. Two others can't outrun a fat man. That leaves only two possible horses that can win, in addition to our horse. We stop the other two, and *Madonna*! We got the only possible winner. Process of elimination."

It was now clear why, among other possible reasons, Trombatore and Tanzini had been in Lafayette for so long. "Are you sure the stuff will work?" I asked.

"We're hitting them with shit that will stop a freight train. Our horse wins, goes clean to the spit box, the two we drug go back to their barns without a test, and that's it. We use exacta and daily double bets so the win odds don't come down and draw the suspicion of the stewards and track security."

"Can they track the horse's connections back to us?"

"Fuck no. The horse is owned and trained by a local yokel Coon-ass who don't know the war is over. He won't be able to tell them shit because he'll be the most surprised sonofabitch at the track."

"Maybe the second most surprised, behind the jockey."

Tanzini grinned. The scheme was quite clever. Racing commissions spent fortunes on devising drug tests for winning horses, and even sent the second place finisher for testing in case he came up just a little short after being hopped or given painkillers. The flaw in their system was that no other horses were tested. Drugging the front runners out of contention was ingenious. By the time the racing officials found out what happened, *if* they ever did, the drugs would be worn off and out of the horses' systems. And, no matter how many questions were asked of the owners, trainers, and jockeys, they truthfully wouldn't know a thing about what happened. Nobody would know how it was pulled off. Except us.

CHAPTER 25

I ran all the scenarios through my head. The scheme would work unless it was botched in the administration of the drugs. "It'll work if the right stuff is used on the right horses," I told Tanzini.

"We're way ahead of you. Here's where you come in."

"One of the two horses we're gonna stop is shipping in from an off-track training center. I'm taking care of him myself. The other horse is stabled on the backstretch. I can't be seen or caught anywhere in the restricted areas. Cabbage Boy knows the barn and stall number where he's stabled. He'll hit him with the shit, but obviously it's a two man job. Waddaya say?"

I wanted to ask him if Trombatore knew about the stratagem, but couldn't. That question would be quite suspect, and besides, we both already knew the obvious answer. I turned my direction to Cabbage Boy and asked Tanzini, "You trust this little asshole?" Cabbage Boy remained cool and didn't flinch in his chair.

"*Non con tutti,*" he answered. "Not with everything, but we've used him before. He knows the horse, his location, and how to administer the shit. He's also the guy who can get you in and out back there at night. He's hit horses with joy juice before, now he gets a chance to make 'em go in the opposite direction. He won't bet. I'll take care of him out of our end."

"If he's okay with you, I'm in." I wretched at the idea of working with the likes of Cabbage Boy, then thought about Tanzini, and figured I couldn't get any dirtier than I already was.

"This stuff maxes out after eighteen hours, so it's got to go down tonight. Our horse is in the second race tomorrow night, post time around seven-thirty. It's after midnight, so we've got to hit these horses in the next couple of hours."

There was no time for me to consult with Lyle or anyone up the ATF chain on whether or not to participate. Besides, it took only a minute to figure out that I couldn't afford not to go along. Busting up the scheme would probably expose me as an undercover agent and jeopardize the Duplessis contract. I went back to the Plantation and changed into jeans and a dark shirt. I secured a black leather ankle holster around my lower leg with the velcro tab and slid my snub-nose in place. I jotted some notes about my activities for the night in case something went wrong, and left them on the desk in my room. If I returned without incident they would probably be torn up and rewritten. If I didn't return, Lyle would have an idea where to look for me in the event I got arrested, or worse.

I parked in a dark spot at the little-used end of a parking lot on the west side of the racetrack. There was only a slither of a moon and the usual humidity was replaced by drier, cooler air that signified rain was on the way. The large oak trees lining the parking lot shuffled from the breezes blown up from the direction of the Gulf of Mexico. I wore sneakers and quietly walked a couple hundred yards in the darkness around the outside perimeter of the eight-foot chain link fence that encased the stable area. The ground was marshy and in spots contained small pools of water. Cabbage Boy waited for me at a pre-designated, secluded location on the inside of the galvanized chain link fence, which was spiked every three inches at the top.

"Psssst!"

The sound coming from the other side of the fence startled me. Cabbage Boy pressed the button on a small penlight pointed at me, which flashed for a fraction of a second. He pointed up to the spikes on top of the fence, and threw a dark gray blanket over the top to make it easier for me to climb over the spikes. It became clear that I wasn't the first person he had sneaked over that fence in the dead of night. I landed with a squishy plop next to him on the inside. I followed his lead as we crept along the fence to the edge of a barn, the first in a long phalanx of identical wooden buildings that each housed eighty horses, forty stalls facing each way back-to-back, with a covered shed-row wrapped around the building. One by one we passed through the shed-rows, darkened and amazingly quiet, considering the hundreds of horses stabled in the area.

"Two more down," he whispered, with a pointed finger.

I was crouched behind him at the corner of a barn, and tapped him on the shoulder as a wobbly shape appeared in the shadows. The figure carried a glass bottle with only a couple of ounces of red wine swishing around the bottom as he staggered toward us. Cabbage Boy hit him with a beam from the penlight. Bloodshot eyes squinted through a wrinkled, reddened face. "It's only old Bimmy," he said quietly. "Gimme a hand."

I set the wine bottle down and we carried the old man to a tack room at the opposite side of the barn. Using only the light available from the sparse street lights at the end of the barn, Cabbage Boy removed a key from the end of a chain clamped onto Bimmy's belt loop, and opened a padlock outside the tack room door. We laid him onto a cot sandwiched between two stacks of alfalfa, and he immediately passed out. A small supply of raggedy clothes and a hotplate confirmed that this was Bimmy's home.

We continued our slink along the buildings to the one with a large number six painted on it. We crept on hands and knees to the middle of the shed-row, and Cabbage Boy stopped short in front of stall number twenty-two. "This is it," he whispered. A bay gelding at least seventeen hands tall, with red liniment bandages arranged neatly on his front legs, stood behind the upper half of the Dutch door. I slid the bolt securing the door and Cabbage Boy crawled into the stall. I followed behind, and shuffled the straw bedding under my feet. I grabbed the horse's halter, which hung on a nail outside his stall, and slipped it onto his head and buckled it. Cabbage Boy handed me the penlight and pulled a plastic ten milliliter syringe from his back pocket, along with a ballpoint pen that was wrapped in a handkerchief. "Gimme some light," he said.

I held the horse in place by his halter when he let out a loud snort, and a spray of mucus landed on my chest.

"Goddamnit," I muttered. I was distracted only momentarily, then directed the light down on Cabbage Boy's hands. He unscrewed the ballpoint pen, which was empty except for a needle. He screwed the needle onto the end of the syringe, which contained a thick, clear liquid.

"Muscle or vein?" I asked.

"Neck shot."

I pointed the thin beam of light at the upper side of the horse's neck. Cabbage Boy placed his thumb deeply into the slight crevice of the neck, several inches below the jaw, and the horse's jugular vein bulged from the pressure. He punctured the skin and stuck the needle upward and into the horse's vein. He extracted a few drops of blood that appeared in the syringe and colored the mixture pink, then shot the entire contents slowly into the vein. We waited for a minute with Cabbage Boy's thumb pressed against the puncture hole to prevent any blood spot. The horse's coat easily concealed the needle hole. I removed the halter and we crawled back out of the stall. I hung the halter back on its nail, and the Dutch door creaked as Cabbage Boy slowly closed and bolted it.

We began our way back to the fence, and crept through the darkness one barn at a time. As we passed one of the many large steel dumpster bins, placed parallel to each barn to collect horse manure and soiled bedding straw, Cabbage Boy tossed the syringe and needle into the bin. Several barns further, closer to the fence, a pair of headlights appeared on the road between the rows of stables. The shell surface crunched beneath the tires of the slow moving vehicle with Evangeline Downs Security painted on the door. We hunkered down behind one of the dumpsters and froze. A bright searchlight beam from the car panned our area slowly, then back again, then abruptly went out. The car made its way to the end of the road where it dead-ended at a locked gate, then turned around and headed back to the guard shack, occasionally shining its beam along the edge of the buildings.

A few small raindrops came down on us as we reached the part of the fence where Cabbage Boy left the blanket. He threw it back over the spikes on the fence, and cupped his hands to give me a boost. The rain fell harder, and thunder rolled in the distance as I climbed back over to the outside of the fence. Cabbage Boy slithered back to his quarters in one of the tack rooms, and since I was now drenched, I didn't hurry my walk back to the car. I threw my shirt, soaked with rain and equine snot, onto the seat and drove back to the Plantation. I dried off, scuttled the notes I had previously written and left on the desk, and replaced them with the shortest note I had ever left for Lyle in the garbage alley: MEET SOON.

I arrived at the clubhouse early, knowing that Tanzini would get there in time to place Daily Double bets using our horse in the second race. Trombatore strode off the escalator with Tanzini in tow, and the maitre 'd escorted them directly to a table. I waved them over to join me, but Trombatore shook his head negatively and sat down. He said something I couldn't hear through the cigarette clenched in his mouth, and motioned Tanzini toward me. The Ice Pick sauntered to my table with an open-collared silk shirt under a tailored sport coat that matched highly polished brown leather shoes. He leaned over a chair across the table and grinned.

"*Va bene?*" he asked.

"Yeah, all is well. How about you?"

"Smooth, a piece of cake. All set. Remember, don't make a win bet."

"My action's already down with a bookie. I might make a few daily doubles."

"*Ciao.*" He walked back to his table, where Trombatore hoisted a glass salute as the waiter brought me a drink with his compliments. He sent the drink to let me know he wasn't snubbing me, yet remained careful not to talk to me. As the second race approached, I studied the Daily Racing Form and watched the horses as they pranced onto the track. Half the field had come over in cold water bandages, indicating their legs were sore puppies. The form's past performances showed that only two horses, numbers one and six, had a chance to win, with our horse, number five, a possibility. The one and six horses were bet heavily from the open, and by post time they were co-favorites at short odds. The five horse was twelve to one on the infield board, a hefty price for a sure thing. The race was for a distance of a mile and forty yards, so the gate crew positioned the starting gate just before the finish line in our line of view. The horses would have to run around the entire track and back again to the finish line. Nothing appeared out of the ordinary in the post parade, and the horses loaded well into the gate. I borrowed a pair of binoculars from a couple having dinner at the table next to me, and looked for stress or fatigue in the horses we had drugged. All seemed normal.

"*Il sont partis!*" trumpeted from the track announcer as the horses made a slow start, normal for a distance race. Number nine, a gray long-shot, took the early lead along the rail. Numbers one and six, our drugged co-favorites, settled in a couple of lengths behind him, and our champion, number five, had only two horses beat around the first turn. Little positioning changed until, as expected, number nine tired after three-quarters of a mile. Numbers six and one, in that order, took the lead by default. In the final turn, number five kept running and broke from the pack of non-runners to ease up into third place. Our horse stormed down the stretch like a stakes horse as the depressants caught up with the front runners. He won by four lengths, and the co-favorites with the load on finished last. The shocked owner and trainer of number five danced and celebrated at the finish line, and glad-handed the jockey as he guided the horse into the winner's circle. By procedure, the winner was sent to the test barn where we knew he would test out okay.

Tanzini winked at me, and Trombatore watched with an uncharacteristic grin as the official results were posted on the tote board. "The results of the second race are official," echoed from the track announcer. Then without warning, Trombatore threw a few bills on the table and they left. They, or rather we, had beaten the spit box, the elaborate drug testing procedure used by every racetrack in America. It was accomplished not by getting stimulants or painkillers past the screen, but by getting slow-down juice past the test to alter the outcome of a race. We had made a textbook score. We fixed a race, and I imagined the pain of every bookmaker and layoff man in New Orleans.

CHAPTER 26

"It's raining so hard the dogs can drink standing up," Ritmo quipped. He was in a good mood. It was late afternoon and had been raining all day. I dropped in The Gallop for the first time since I made the buy from Dubroc and Tanzini. I knew that if the deal with Frank Duplessis concluded the next day, this could be my last trip to the place.

"What's cooking, Ritmo?"

"I've got something to show you," he beamed. He hurriedly wiped his hands on a bar towel and took me through the rear door of the club. A sheet of water fell from the small overhang above the back door. Parked a few feet away was a brand new, wine-colored Mercedes-Benz coupe. "I've gotta build a carport back here for it. Nice wheels, huh Tony?"

"Yeah. Beautiful."

"I've got you to thank for it."

Ritmo had used his share of the money from the bank securities as a down payment on the car. The color of the vehicle seemed appropriate since it was literally bought with blood money. The car purchase meant that some, if not all of Uncle Sam's one-hundred thousand dollars in buy money had slipped through the surveillance.

"I'm glad for you, Ritmo. I guess Cliff bought one too."

"Hell, no. He's already got a big hog. Besides, he's got too much Cajun blood in him to spend this much at one time."

I pushed him for more information about the connection between Phil Tanzini and The Gallop. "Why didn't you tell me about Tanzini?"

"I don't fuck with that guy. Period. I can put two and two together, but I don't know much about him and Cliff or what they do. I don't wanna know." He was lying.

"Why the dumb act?"

"Look, a few times I gave him cash envelopes from Cliff. I never looked inside."

It became obvious that I wasn't going to get any more out of him. I changed the subject. "Where is Cheri's day job? I need to talk to her."

Ritmo perked up. "Come on, I'll take you for a ride in the Benz, we'll go there." We finished a drink together, then climbed into his new car. He drove downtown and parked directly in front of a small office building that spelled out Mouton Insurance Agency in gold lettering on the plate glass window. Inside, a well-dressed receptionist sat behind a long desk. Before I could ask for Cheri I heard small steps clacking towards me on the hard terrazzo floor. Cheri was dressed in a tight navy skirt and white blouse, with attractive but inexpensive jewelry around her neck. She also wore a big smile.

"Did you get lost, *Cher*?"

"Maybe so. Guess I'm in the wrong place." I turned my back to her and took a step toward the door. She grabbed me by the arm. "Okay, okay. Two can tease. Would you like a soda?"

"Sure."

I followed her into the small break room and sat down. She got two soda cans from a small refrigerator and sat down next to me. "I can take my break now, but I only have a few minutes. I'm glad you came by, but why didn't you let me know you were back before now?"

"I've been busy."

"So I heard."

"Heard? Heard what?"

"Never mind."

"How about dinner tonight?"

Her smile widened for a moment, then she got a sour look on her face. "I can't. It's Friday night, I'm working."

"No you're not. I fixed it with Ritmo. I'll pick you up at eight. The smile returned, and she leaned over and kissed me on the cheek. She scribbled her address on an insurance agency note pad and jumped up from her chair.

"I'll be ready," she said. "Can you find your way out?"

I joined Ritmo, who was still admiring the new car from his position behind the steering wheel. He headed back to the club and said, "Cliff's been asking for you. Are you coming back tonight?"

"Maybe."

I listened to the news from the radio on the night table in my room. A large turnout was expected for the Louisiana primary elections the following day. I thought about the date with Cheri. I probably wouldn't see her again after that night. I was near the end of the investigation in Lafayette, so it was harmless to socialize with her now, at least as far as the case was concerned. But, any intimacy with her was cheating on Gina. Or was it? After all, I had been literally thrown out of my house. The ink wasn't yet dry on the divorce petition Gina filed against me. I was still married, but only by means of legal technicality.

I easily found the small rental cottage located on a tree-lined street in the city. When I arrived, the screen door swung open and Cheri turned to the little girl with the blonde ringlets who was held by the babysitter. She blew a kiss and said, "Be good, Monique. Go to sleep when it's time." She skipped to the car and let herself in. Before I could restart the engine she put her hand around the back of my neck and pulled me toward her. She gave me a long, deep, soul-searing kiss. I hadn't been kissed like that for months and had forgotten how good it felt. Then she sat straight up and said, "Where to?"

We arrived at Prejean's, one of the finest restaurants in town. I could tell she hadn't spent much time in this kind of establishment. The lighting was subdued, and soft music drifted from the piano bar. The place was cozy and classy. We were shown to our table by a tuxedo clad maitre d' who delivered the wine list and menu.

"Order anything you want," I said.

"Anything?" She giggled, but ordered in French as soon as the waiter arrived.

We ate leisurely and had several glasses of wine. We held hands across the table, which was covered with a brown linen tablecloth. I told her how I respected her for holding two jobs while caring for her child, all while avoiding the traps and pitfalls associated with The Gallop and its clientele. I knew that indictments against Cliff, Ritmo, and Tanzini were being drawn up as we spoke. The Gallop would probably be padlocked within days and she wouldn't have the second job. But I couldn't tell her that.

"Stay with your day job, Cheri. Go back to school, at night if you have to. Get away from Ritmo and the rest of those assholes."

"Assholes? They're your pals, not mine. I just work there."

She was right. It felt good knowing that she thought that way. Before I could go further with my little speech, she stopped me in my tracks. She leaned forward and said in a soft voice, "I can't see you anymore, Tony."

I sat back in surprise and let her continue.

"I meet a lot of guys, especially in the club. I've stayed away from all of them. I was making an exception for you. But I've been told you're bad news and to stay away from you."

I looked closely into her eyes and for the first time I sensed fear in them. There were still flashes of kindness and interest, but the fear came through.

"Don't listen to Cliff and Ritmo," I told her. "Cliff and Ritmo?" she laughed. "They love you."

"Then who warned you?"

"Uncle Frank."

"Uncle Frank?"

"Duplessis. The horse trainer. He's the serious one in the family and when he speaks, we listen. He warned me, told me you're an ex-con. I had already figured that out for myself and it didn't bother me. Then he told me that you're a killer." She stopped talking and waited for a reply - a denial, a laugh, any kind of response.

I was stunned. The whole time that I had been working to gain enough confidence from Duplessis to give me the murder contract, I was befriending his niece. Any slip around her would have been disastrous in more ways than one. "He hardly knows me. What else did he tell you about me?"

"Nothing. He's a man of few words. But he's looked out for me since I was a teenager, when my dad died. He's not my real uncle, he's my *parrain*, my Godfather. He was my dad's best friend." She put her head down. "I can't see you anymore. But I wanted us to have tonight." She looked up at me with a question in her eyes that now brightened. She once again wanted me to spend the night with her. A one time, parting fling. But her sudden revelation was my way out, my way to break it off with her.

I tried to sound convincing.

"Tonight's already history," I told her. "I'm not good enough for a long haul but okay for a farewell fuck. I guess you come down as just another bitch along life's path. I'm taking you home."

We drove back to her house in silence, except for her low sobs. This innocent girl's feelings were hurt, another casualty left in the wake of my investigation. Did she cry from the insult, or from ending a relationship that never really began? Before she went inside we kissed, this time for several minutes. Then she pushed me away and was gone.

Lyle had warned me months ago that most of the half-million Cajuns in Louisiana were related in some kind of way, if not by blood, then by marriage or social setting. I had no idea Cheri was related to any of the subjects of our investigation, much less Duplessis.

In a few days, when the arrests were made and I was far away out of the cold, she would know the truth. I wouldn't be Tony, the low-life killer. But I would be Tony the rat, Tony the fink, Tony the fed. Tony, the guy who put the uncle who tried to protect her in the slammer. She would also know that the insults I gave her were scripted. At least, I hoped so.

CHAPTER 27

Lyle and I sat in a corner of Jean Lafitte's. The nightclub was named for the most infamous pirate of the south Louisiana bayous and was a popular watering hole. The richly grained mahogany bar was built around a scale model of Lafitte's pirate ship, complete with the skull and crossbones of the Jolly Roger. The cavernous place was darkly lit in keeping with the pirate motif. I told Lyle some of the conversation I had with Cheri just hours earlier. He took a large swallow from a longneck beer. "Ah, the old Coon-ass connection. I warned you about that. If I looked hard enough I might be related to Duplessis myself," he laughed.

"Did you find Cabbage Boy's syringe? What drug was in it?"

"We found it all right. We had the waste company tow the dumpster you described to the middle of a rice field and empty it. Then three other agents and myself picked through two tons of horse shit, handful by handful. One of our federal shit diggers was a rookie, hasn't even been to T-school yet, just sworn in last week. His first assignment in a big-time federal case was sifting through a bin of horse shit."

I smiled and slapped at the table. "Helluva letdown for the kid after being pumped up about his importance from the recruiting films."

"Don't laugh. Do you have any idea how many flies hover around two tons of horse shit? Not your average housefly, but those big, green, nasty bastards that sting – horseflies. Not to mention the smell."

"Did you send the syringe to the lab?"

"Sure did, shipped it to Washington this morning." Lyle looked down and said in a softer voice, "Along with the five other needles and syringes we found in the bin."

"You mean there were six needle and syringe outfits in that bin?"

"Affirmative. That dumpster is emptied twice a week, so imagine how much of that crap is out there. And, there's more than fifty of them on the backstretch, we only emptied one of them. Do you think some of those outfits are legitimate, throwaways from veterinarians?"

"No way. The vets collect their sharps, they don't throw them into shit bins." I slumped in the chair, disappointed at the news. No matter what the ATF lab found in those syringes, the evidence was useless. There was no way to single out one of the six outfits found in a large dumpster, and pin it on Cabbage Boy. No competent prosecutor would present a case on my testimony alone without credible physical evidence to corroborate. With no case on Cabbage Boy, there was no drug or race fixing case on Phil Tanzini. And of course, linking Luke Trombatore was a total pipe dream.

Our attention turned to the matter at hand, and Lyle gave me the background on Duplessis' intended victims. Antoine Broussard was the largest cattle rancher in the area. He lived in the mansion-styled home in Crowley, but owned hundreds of acres of cattle land and rice fields. More important to his source of wealth were the oil and gas leases on his land, a lucrative commodity in southwest Louisiana. Broussard was on the board of directors of a local bank, owned majority interest in a supermarket, and was well respected in the community. He was a civic-minded poll inspector, was chairman of the Democratic party for Acadia Parish, and a member of the state central committee of that party. He was a widower whose daughter was a student at LSU, attending a summer study program in Europe.

Danielle Duplessis had been a faithful wife to Frank for over twenty years. She had taught elementary school in their early years together but gave it up at Frank's insistence. They had no children, and she had put all her effort into caring for him and their home. She had lived a quiet life except for the occasional beatings administered by her husband. Despite the abuse, she had never left him. But one night several months earlier, she seized the opportunity when he threw her clothes into the front yard of their house in a fit of rage. She moved in with her elderly parents, and shortly afterward began dating Broussard. They had been sweethearts in high school but eventually married other people. The relationship rekindled after Broussard learned of Danielle's separation from Frank. She had recently updated her teaching certificate and was set to begin a new life. Like Antoine Broussard, Danielle had no idea of Frank's scheme.

I told Lyle of my plan to convince Duplessis at our meeting the following night that I had carried out his murder contract. "The sheriff in Acadia Parish is a standup guy, right?" I asked.

"That's right. Elton Arceneaux has been sheriff for a long time and we've worked closely with him for years. We've never detected corruption in his department. The same goes for the District Attorney's office."

"Longtime sheriff... that means he should know a man of Broussard's stature quite well."

"Undoubtedly."

"Good. Here's the plan. We need a surveillance team on Broussard and Danielle all day tomorrow."

"They're already in place," Lyle interrupted. "The boys in D.C. had a shit fit when they found out about Broussard's political clout. They wanted him tailed for protection in case Frank got anxious and jumped the gun."

"Okay, so that's in place. Put a team on Danielle also. About an hour before my scheduled meeting with Frank, you and Sheriff Arceneaux intercept them. Explain the situation and get Broussard's wallet, his identification, and his wristwatch. Also, get me a personal item from Danielle. Turn them over to me, and I'll deliver them to Frank as proof I killed him and beat her up. After he pays me, you can close in."

"I think it'll work. The only problem may be resistance from Broussard. He'll be a busy guy and eager to get to his party headquarters after the polls close."

"Resistance? He's got no choice. Put his ass in protective custody if you have to."

"Calm down, will you? Between the sheriff and me I'm sure we can get him to cooperate."

"What about the indictments on Cliff and the gang?"

"The grand jury handed down sealed indictments on Cliff, Ritmo, and Tanzini. We're holding their warrants until this is over. We'll pick them up after we bust Frank."

Election morning was a hectic one for Antoine Broussard. He met with his precinct captains an hour before the polls opened at six o'clock. He had a balancing act to perform. He coordinated the effort to get out the Cajun vote that had been populist in nature since the days of Huey Long. He also worked as an unbiased poll inspector. He bustled to and from the various voting precincts, assuring that no problems occurred and that election laws were carried out. He did so all day long, oblivious to the ATF agents who followed his every move.

I spent part of that afternoon at The Gallop. Ritmo was still crowing about his new Mercedes Bentz and wanted my opinion on his putting spoke wire wheels on the car. "Sure, Ritmo. Why not? Then it will look like a real pimpmobile." He sneered at me from under his off-center toupee'. At this point, I really didn't care if I insulted him or pissed him off.

"Why are you busting my balls, Tony?"

"Forget it. You said Cliff wanted to see me?"

He walked to the spot behind the bar where the buzzer to Cliff Dubroc's office was located, and pushed the button. Within a minute, Cliff appeared in the office doorway and viewed the club in his usual manner. He wore gray pleated pants and a starched, light blue shirt. His demeanor again reminded me that he could be dropped into a college classroom and be mistaken for a lecturer on Roman civilization. I also knew that within hours he and Ritmo would be in custody and transported to a more exclusive institution, at least until he made bail.

Cliff went behind the bar and poured himself a shot of Black Jack, then leaned over toward me. "Are you interested in some more swag? If so, come back tonight," he said.

"You know the answer to that . . . it all depends." We had all we needed on Cliff, but I had to maintain the role and hoped to get more information on Phil Tanzini and the long-shot possibility of linking his boss, Luke Trombatore, to the securities case.

"I haven't seen the Ice Pick lately. Is he in town or back in New Orleans?"

He laughed and looked at me from his eyes above the small glasses now set far down on the bridge of his nose.

"He's waaaaaaaay out of town. England, I heard."

"England?" I couldn't hide the surprise in my voice.

"Yeah. Go figure. I guess he's cooling out from who-knows-what."

Ritmo joined us, and the rest of the conversation was small talk about the election. This was the last time they would know me as Tony Parrino. Before I left, I couldn't resist a parting shot at them both. "Hey, Cliff, why don't you get off a dime and give Ritmo a raise so he can replace that cheap fucking muskrat on his head?"

Election Tuesday...

Voter turnout was heavy, but the machine counting allowed the poll commissioners to complete their evening tally shortly after the eight o'clock closing time. Antoine Broussard's official duties were finished. He picked up Danielle from her home and drove directly to his house to freshen up before going to party headquarters to await the election results. His movements were exactly as Frank Duplessis had described. He pulled his car into the carport adjacent to his house when Lyle and Sheriff Arceneaux approached him. Arceneaux greeted him and Danielle, and introduced Lyle Melancon as an ATF agent. Broussard was startled, and asked why the sheriff himself and a federal agent would visit his home. He relaxed slightly when Lyle answered him in French. They told him there was urgent business at hand, and that he and Danielle were needed back at the sheriff's office immediately. Within a minute they were whisked away.

Lyle went directly to a rendezvous spot on a side road about three miles from the Blue Goose in Rayne. He handed me a rich alligator-skin wallet containing the driver's license and other effects of Antoine Broussard, along with a Rolex President wristwatch and a gold crucifix attached to a gold neck chain. He also gave me a small scented handkerchief embroidered in red around the edges and with the initials "DD" in one corner. I wrapped the items in the handkerchief and slipped them into my coat pocket.

"Did Broussard give you any trouble?"

"No, it went pretty smooth. But he's scared out of his mind. So is Danielle. They're on ice in the sheriff's office."

A voice transmission came over Lyle's radio to let him know Frank Duplessis was at The Blue Goose. "The subject has arrived." He acknowledged the message, then turned to me.

"That's it. Get over there and put this baby to sleep." We reached out and shook hands and the feel of the familiar bear paw wrapped around my fingers was reassuring. I started to leave when Lyle took a small glass jar from a paper bag. He dipped his fingertips in it and flicked his fingers toward me. I flinched as several small crimson droplets splashed onto my white shirt and dark blue coat. "Chicken blood," he said. "I had T-Red come up with this. He's scratching his ass wondering why. Nice effect."

Frank Duplessis was seated in his truck in the rear parking lot of the Blue Goose. Unlike our first meeting there, he was prompt, maybe because he was anxious. I parked directly behind him to block any quick escape in the event that something went awry. I got into the passenger side slowly, and held the door open for a few seconds so the dome light would help him notice the blood on my clothes.

He eyes went straight to the red dots splattered against my white shirt.

"He's dead. Let's make it quick, Frank." I reached into my pocket and threw the personal effects of Broussard and Danielle in his lap. He opened the wallet and thumbed through the I.D., credit cards, and family photos, straining because of the limited light. He slowly examined the Rolex and gold religious article, and a sardonic smile came to his face, the same eerie look he got when he gave me the orders to kill. He put Broussard's objects down when he recognized the handkerchief. He held it up to the dim light, then drew it to his face with both hands and breathed in it's scent. The twisted smile was replaced by a worried look.

"You didn't kill her, did you?"

"No. But she's busted up, needs stitches. Ain't that what you wanted?

He grunted and nodded his head affirmatively. Then he leaned over the steering wheel and reached to the left under the dashboard. I instinctively put my hand on the butt of my gun, which was stuck in the front of my waistband. He fidgeted under the dash for a few seconds and removed a small package that had been taped underneath and handed it to me. It was a neat stack of hundred dollar bills bound by bank wrappers, the same size and type he paid me with a few days earlier.

I put the package into my inside coat pocket, when Duplessis suddenly wheeled toward me with a double-barreled sawed-off shotgun and shoved the barrels up against my left temple. The cold steel against my head seemed to freeze my whole body. Blood rushed to my head so fast that I could feel and hear the throbs in my ears. My hand was still on my gun but was useless against a weapon that could take my head off with the slightest touch. So many thoughts flooded my mind, in rapid succession.

Was this how it ended? Do I die at the hands of a madman caught up in a love triangle? Surely there were more gallant ways for an ATF agent to go out. I thought about not having a wire on me, how it might have brought help. But would it? If the surveillance agents close-by knew there was a gun propped against my head and they charged the scene, any nervous reaction by Duplessis, any slight movement, would kill me. Inexplicably, my thoughts turned to the classroom of my Catholic grammar school, to the words of Sister Catherine teaching the act of contrition, which cleanses the soul before death. But I didn't say that prayer. Instead, the words of the Hail Mary that we recited so repetitively in the Rosary as kids seemed to pour out into my mind. I hoped to complete the mental prayer before he pulled the trigger. The quick prayer helped me gain control of my thoughts.

Where did the sawed-off come from? Duplessis obviously had it hidden between him and the door out of my sight. My instincts had been correct to grab my gun when he reached forward, but I relaxed for just a second when the object he reached for turned out to be money. In that split second he got the advantage. These thoughts all flooded over me in a matter of only a few seconds. I was physically and mentally braced for whatever death brings. Then I began to think rationally, and gained control of the thought process. If he intended to kill me, would he do it in a public place? A double-barreled sawed-off would literally blow my brains out. Would he do that in his own vehicle? Not likely. And if he was robbing me, why did he pay me in the first place? He had to have something else in mind, and this bolstered me. I didn't move a muscle and kept looking straight ahead, but said in the calmest, harshest voice I could muster, "What the fuck is this? Are you ripping me off? Why didn't you just keep the money?"

"Fuck the money. I just want you to listen, and listen good." His voice was slow and deliberate, as if he had practiced what he said. "Leave T-Red alone."

"T-Red?"

"You said you had to kill him because he put us together. He's a pain in the ass little bastard but he don't deserve to die. Leave him alone."

Duplessis then lowered the shotgun and placed it in his lap. That quickly, it was over. My hand was still on my gun and I could have killed him - justifiably. But something told me he was no longer an immediate threat, just a sick individual. I broke open the shotgun, ejected the two twelve-gauge shells and put them in my coat pocket, then threw the shotgun back in his lap. Then I wasted no time getting out of the truck. However, before I closed the door, I looked him in the eye and said, "See you in hell, Frank."

I left Broussard's property and Danielle's handkerchief with him to be recovered as evidence in his possession. I tore out of the parking lot without giving the surveillance agents the headlight signal to move in. I drove to the rendezvous spot and waited for Lyle. He pulled his G-car in the opposite direction of mine and rolled down the window. "No go?" he asked.

"Yeah, it's done. But the motherfucker has a sawed-off, and I didn't want you guys going in on him without warning."

"We'll handle it. I'll meet you at the Plantation."

My delay in signaling gave Duplessis the opportunity to get out of the parking lot of the Blue Goose. A few miles away he was overtaken by the surveillance teams and was taken down without incident.

CHAPTER 28

I stretched out on my back across the bed, rubbed my eyes, and quietly waited for my blood pressure to return to normal. The silence ended with a knock on the door. "Nice place you have here," Lyle said sarcastically as he entered. "What a pit." During the whole time I lived there he had never seen my room, never even been inside or around the hotel except to retrieve my notes from the garbage alley.

"Welcome to my castle. Now you know why I spent so much time in The Gallop. Classier place." He set two cups of strong coffee on the small table in the corner of the room. "I guess it's over, now that I'm drinking coffee instead of Bloody Marys."

"Not quite. The sheriff has asked you to come to his office. Broussard and Danielle are quite upset and somewhat in disbelief. He'd like you to talk to them, a horse's mouth sort of thing."

"I can't talk about the case with them, Lyle, you know that. Can't you handle it? I've had enough for one day."

He glanced down into the cup containing the dark pool of coffee and said, "We owe it to the sheriff. We dumped all this crap in his jurisdiction on short notice to get it out of St. Landry Parish."

He was right. I took off the blood-stained shirt and changed into a clean one. Before we left I asked him about Duplessis. "The sawed-off was reloaded," he answered. "He was plenty surprised when we pulled him over. He offered no resistance, but kept asking what it was all about. We didn't tell him shit. Let him find out at the arraignment."

"That prick. He didn't intend to kill me, only throw a scare into me. But if he had moved just to slap a mosquito I'd be dead. Make sure to add assault to his charges."

"We can't."

"What?"

"To charge assault on a federal officer we have to prove he knew you were a fed. Picture this. Defense attorney in court: "How could he possibly know you were a federal officer when, according to you, he just paid you to commit murder?"

"Shit. You're right."

We went through a private entrance to Sheriff Arceneaux's office where he waited for us. The room looked more like the den of a hunting lodge than the executive office of a police agency. Behind a huge desk was a stone hearth fireplace. Above the mantle stared the fierce yellow eyes of a mounted swamp wildcat, with a perpetual growl showing long, gnarled teeth. A small alligator head sat on the desk. The room was cozy, with several plush chairs and a large sofa that all faced the fireplace. The only reminders that this was a law enforcement office were a glass-enclosed gun rack on the wall and several sharpshooting trophies on the coffee table.

Arceneaux greeted us warmly. He was a short, stout man in his sixties with neatly combed gray hair. He wore leather cowboy boots below his starched khaki pants and a brown plaid cowboy shirt. He spoke with the same thick Cajun accent as the other bayou natives. After he offered a firm handshake he got quickly got to the point. "Good to know you, son. I've got some very scared citizens in the next room. They're also puzzled and don't know what to believe. Can you help me?"

"I'll meet with them but can't give particulars of the case until it's disposed of in court."

"I understand," he said. He left us in the room alone and went to get Broussard and Danielle.

Lyle sat unevenly on the edge of the big desk with one leg dangling and the other on the floor. We looked around the office and he said, "The high sheriff in a place like this is more than the law. He knows most of the people and has to be their friend, advisor, arbitrator, and sometimes their confessor, besides being their sheriff. We'll be out of here in a few days, but he has to stay and deal with the fallout. He wants these people to know he didn't cook up Frank's arrest, that it was our case."

A moment later Arceneaux returned with the intended victims. Antoine Broussard was strikingly neat, with dark wavy hair and a darker complexion than most Cajuns. He was in his mid-forties without a wrinkle in his face. He walked in with a small radio in his hand, and occasionally placed it to his ear as if he was keeping up with the score of a football game. He was listening for election results. Danielle Duplessis was a thin, small-framed woman with short, dark hair and green eyes emphasized by red, puffy eyelids from crying.

Both of them fixed their eyes on me as the sheriff explained that Frank hired me to kill Broussard in front of Danielle. Their blank expression became a probing stare.

"Sheriff Arceneaux didn't know anything about this until today," I told them. "I can't give you any details right now but you should know, that had Frank reached a true killer before he reached me, you would be dead, Mr. Broussard."

"Oh, my God," Danielle whispered.

Broussard put his radio down and held her. "I don't know whether to thank you or curse you," he said. He asked several concise questions, which Lyle and the sheriff answered. But they really weren't there to ask questions, just to get a look at the man who was supposed to commit this heinous act, this killer-federal agent. The brief meeting satisfied them, although they seemed more despondent, more resolved to the situation after we met. The sheriff escorted them from the office into a long, well-lit hallway. As he held the door open for them, Broussard turned back toward me for a moment. He started to speak, but hesitated and gave me a simple nod. I knew what he meant.

Through the open door I got a glimpse of the long hallway and a room at the end of it. Frank Duplessis stood in the room as an officer removed the handcuffs from behind his back and began to fingerprint him. The sheriff returned and thanked us. He and Lyle had a brief, back-slapping conversation in French, then he broke into English for the benefit of us both. "Payoffs and crooked deals have been a way of life here since the ink was still wet on the Louisiana Purchase. Being an honest sheriff and getting re-elected don't go together. But here I am, socializing with the feds." We laughed.

I couldn't wait to get back to my room. I threw my clothes on the floor and got in the shower. The hottest water that would come out of the old pipes cascaded down my body. I soaped from scalp to feet. In what had become a ritual at the end of every undercover assignment, I scrubbed away the stale smoke and smells associated with the case. It had the effect of washing away The Gallop, Frank Duplessis, Cliff Dubroc, Ritmo Angelle, Phil Tanzini, Luke Trombatore, Cabbage Boy, and the other undesirable characters and places that had become part of my life. I stayed there for what seemed like an hour until the water ran cold.

Two days later I packed my things and loaded up the Camaro. The drizzly, damp weather would slow the normal two hour drive to New Orleans. As I leaned over to place a briefcase on the floorboard, there was a tap on my behind accompanied by T-Red's voice. "Bugging out on me?"

"Hell, yeah."

"Will you be back?"

"Only if I'm needed in court."

T-Red leaned against the car and crossed his legs. "It's been fun, ain't it?

"Let's put it this way, Red. Everybody's gotta be someplace."

"Well, it hasn't been a thrill for me either. But we're both still here, with our asses in one piece. That's something." His tone was as dreary as the weather.

"I wish I could have cut you out sooner, but we never know how it's going to play out. If you keep your mouth shut, nobody will know you were involved. We're not even giving your name to the DA."

"I figured I could count on that." His voice perked up. "Hey, Tony, too bad you're leaving town. Delta Downs opens next week and I've been galloping an old cockroach of a horse that'll go off at twenty to one. He'll win."

I looked down into the tiny man's eyes set against his ruddy face. "Here's a yard. Bet it for yourself," I told him. He took the hundred-dollar bill with a grin, then he grabbed me by the forearms and gripped them tightly. I returned the gesture. "What am I supposed to do you little bastard, kiss you goodbye?" He bent over laughing. He walked through the light mist to his old, dilapidated pickup truck that was parked several spaces away. I noticed two small children, a boy and girl about the same age, seated in the truck. Two more boys, pre-teens, one slightly older and bigger than the other, sat in the bed of the truck just behind the cab. The children were dressed in worn clothes, and all four had the same thick, reddish-brown hair as T-Red.

I had spent the better part of a year with this man who, regardless of his motives, risked his life alongside mine, and had never known he had a family. Never even asked. For that matter, never cared. It struck me that if Duplessis had taken my head off, or Tanzini had stuck a shiv in me, or any other peril had befallen me, at least my family would have a government pension and insurance to fall back on. If T-Red had met the same fate, his innocent, unwitting kids would have gotten *zip*. I swung my car around and called out to him. He walked over to the window, and I reached into my pocket and grabbed whatever bills were in it. Without counting it I stuffed all the money I had into his shirt pocket. I made a gesture toward the children in the truck and said, "Bet it on them."

I never saw T-Red again.

The windshield wipers slowly slapped time. The radio announced that President Gerald Ford had gotten more Republican votes than California governor Ronald Reagan in the Louisiana primary, and Jimmy Carter had edged out the shortened list of Democrats. Antoine Broussard had delivered Acadia Parish. Traffic thickened in the arteries leading to downtown as the New Orleans skyline became visible above the misty haze. I drove into the basement parking facility of the federal building and went directly to the ATF conference room.

The room was chilly and felt even colder because of the damp weather. Lyle sat in a chair at the long table and busily thumbed through notes on a tablet. Without looking up he said, "The crew from Washington is here." I sat across from him and listened to the quiet flow of cold air through the air condition vents, interrupted occasionally by a crackling sound each time Lyle turned a page. I thought about the last time I was in this room, when I was given Gina's divorce papers and had exploded. Within a few minutes the heavy door opened and SAC Jim King entered, followed by an attractive young brunette. He introduced her as an investigative assistant and she sat down to take notes. Paul McKinney and Jim Fenton soon followed and took seats at the table.

We exchanged the cursory handshakes, but the air was heavy with weariness. We all were drained from the prolonged case and all that it entailed, and nobody looked forward to the volumes of reports each of us would be writing in the next few days. King conducted the meeting as he and McKinney peppered me with questions, mostly of a technical nature and to prepare court presentation. The debriefing took about an hour, then I was brought up to speed on happenings behind the scenes. King was matter-of-fact in his delivery. "Duplessis is still locked up on a half-million dollars bail. He pled not guilty at his arraignment. No news on whether he'll plea guilty or go to trial. We picked up Ritmo Angelle at The Gallop and Cliff

Dubroc in a Lafayette whorehouse. They also pled not guilty in their case and are awaiting a trial date. Higher bail was set for them but we expect them to post it soon. We can't find Phil Tanzini. We've notified Scotland Yard and Interpol that he may be in England. We've only recovered a small amount of the buy money but we're working on it."

"What about the bank heist?" I asked.

"Nobody's talking. We all think Luke Trombatore was behind it but we don't have shit linking him to it. Tanzini is the buffer and we don't have him. Not much chance of him talking, anyway. The cop killer in custody, James Bratton, won't talk, and his partner is still at large. Even if he did talk, the best he could give us is Tanzini. The electric chair is a better alternative for him than squealing on mob guys."

"Then it's a dead end," I said. "Cliff and Ritmo didn't know where those notes came from. Of course, they didn't care, either. Tanzini was the buffer between them and Trombatore. So, all we've got on them is possession and sale of the stolen securities. So be it."

I stood up to stretch my back and asked, "What about the race fixing case?"

"Well, you know the criminal case went down the tubes," Lyle said. "But we made a referral to the state racing commission as well as all the racing commissions in the country. We don't yet know how much attention they'll give the matter, but the Louisiana commission has begun testing random horses in addition to the winners. Our case will probably reform the industry so far as drug testing racehorses is concerned."

Jim Fenton put down his smoking pipe and handed me a large stack of mail wrapped by several thick rubber bands. Some pieces were a few months old. "Here's your stuff, Tony," he said. "Your new orders are in the blue envelope." I tucked the mail under my arm. Fenton and I shook hands, and we quickly disbanded. There was no fanfare, no "Thank you," no "Well done," no "Go fuck yourself." There hadn't been at the end of any of the previous cases I worked, so I didn't expect as much. It was another day at the office for them.

After the small group exited the conference room, Lyle and I headed to a busy café nearby. He looked at me with an obvious question about my orders. I tore open the blue envelope on top of the stack and shared the news with him. "I'm headed back to my home office in Miami to depressurize for a couple of weeks. After that, I report to the Secret Service detail at the Democratic National Convention in New York."

Lyle was agitated. "Those assholes couldn't let you stay home for a while?" His voice calmed and he said, "If it makes you feel any better, I'm headed to the DNC myself. Maybe we can hook up with Ernie Chinn." He drove me to the airport and walked with me all the way to the gate. The other passengers boarded the plane as Lyle gave me a good-natured but forceful punch on the arm. "You did okay. We gathered enough criminal intelligence to keep law enforcement in Acadiana busy for some time. We also got some bad guys off the street, and you found the assassin. Good thing for all around, it was you."

Assassin Hunter

About the Author

AUGUST PALUMBO is a former New Orleans homicide detective and a retired special agent of the Bureau of Alcohol, Tobacco, Firearms and Explosives. He was awarded the NOPD Medal of Merit and received numerous commendations from the United States Treasury Department for intrepid service, as well as the Distinguished Firearms Expert award.

He holds a Criminology degree from Loyola University New Orleans; and currently serves as a consultant to the National Association of Federal Agents.

Made in the USA
Lexington, KY
07 April 2012